GREAT ROAD STYLE

DEVELOPED BY THE WILLIAM KING REGIONAL ARTS CENTER
IN 1994, THE CULTURAL HERITAGE PROJECT DOCUMENTS
THE ARTISTIC LEGACY OF SOUTHWEST VIRGINIA AND
NORTHEAST TENNESSEE AND SEEKS TO FOSTER A FULL
AND ACCURATE APPRECIATION OF THE REGION'S ROLE
IN AMERICAN DECORATIVE ARTS.

Great Road Style

THE DECORATIVE ARTS LEGACY
OF SOUTHWEST VIRGINIA
AND NORTHEAST TENNESSEE

BETSY K. WHITE

University of Virginia Press Charlottesville and London

Publication of this volume was assisted by a grant from Furthermore:
a program of the J. M. Kaplan Fund, and by a gift in memory of Glenn C. Price.

University of Virginia Press
© 2006 by the Rector and Visitors of the
University of Virginia
Printed in China on acid-free paper

First published 2006

9 8 7 6 5 4 3 2 1

Library of Congress Cataloging-in-Publication Data
White, Betsy K., 1947–
Great road style : the decorative arts legacy of
southwest Virginia and northeast Tennessee /
Betsy K. White.
p. cm.
Includes bibliographical references and index.
ISBN 0-8139-2352-2 (cloth : alk. paper)
1. Decorative arts—Virginia. 2. Decorative arts—
Tennessee. I. Title.
NK1410.V8W49 2006
745'.09755—dc22
        2004028300

Contents

Preface

This book is based upon nine years of research by William King Regional Arts Center into the decorative arts history of Southwest Virginia and Northeast Tennessee—otherwise known as Great Road Style. The project's goal was to broaden the record of objects made by hand in the area prior to 1940 and to develop a representative picture of the region's role in American decorative arts. The first substantive effort to conduct primary research in this largely undocumented area, the survey spanned two states, incorporated rugged geography, and included many isolated communities. The baseline study was planned to last for two years, with an exhibition of representative examples of the items found the anticipated result. The area encompassed the counties of far Southwest Virginia (Buchanan, Dickenson, Lee, Russell, Scott, Smyth, Tazewell, Washington, and Wise) and Northeast Tennessee (Carter, Greene, Hawkins, Johnson, Sullivan, and Washington), places connected historically, culturally, and geographically.

To prepare for this project, and to plan our survey of the region, we met with researchers from the Museum of Early Southern Decorative Arts (MESDA) to study their methodology, searched for any published materials on regional decorative arts, and spoke to anyone we could who had an interest in the subject matter. We began with the few known existing research projects and the resulting literature: a 1971 regional issue of *Antiques* that featured Northeast Tennessee furniture and art as well as an inventory of pre-1840 artisans; a 1972 article on Washington County, Virginia, pottery written for the Historical Society of Washington County by Dr. Klell Napps; a 1983 *Antiques* article by Roddy Moore (a recognized authority on the region's material culture) on earthenware pottery from the region that he referred to as "Great Road Pottery"; and a 1984 *Antiques* article by Moore on regional furniture with pierced-tin panels. In this last article, Moore focused on Wythe County, Virginia, which bordered our survey area. The examples he included provided us with a starting point and a template of sorts for our study of this furniture form within our target counties. We also relied on the 2002 survey of the pottery of Washington County, Virginia (by field researcher Christopher Espenshade of Skelly and Loy, Inc., for the Virginia Department of Historic Resources), an important in-depth report on one county's active pottery industry from its eighteenth-century beginnings to its close around 1900. In addition to these studies, other summary reviews of specific topics existed, often in the few museums that hold objects from the region in their collections or in the work of collectors seeking information on individual pieces.

The primary method of building our new database was to be a door-to-door survey of residences, documenting and photographing all we could find with local provenance made by hand prior to 1940—everything from furniture to pottery, textiles, metalwork, paintings and works on paper, baskets, and musical instruments. In addition, we relied on census records in each of the fifteen survey counties—particularly the 1850 and 1860 censuses that recorded occupations. In selected instances, we turned to earlier and later records as well as newspaper abstracts and advertisements to track down the locations of identified artisans.

Using funds for the project from a 1993 National Endowment for the Arts Advancement Grant, we assembled a group of consulting curators and a full-time field researcher. Roddy Moore, Director of the Blue Ridge Institute at Ferrum College, who had done much of the existing research, was the logical choice as lead consultant. He brought three additional experts to the team: Wallace B. Gusler and

Richard Miller, from Colonial Williamsburg, and Vaughan Webb, Assistant Director at the Blue Ridge Institute. Colleen Callahan, now Curator Emeritus of Costumes and Textiles at the Valentine Richmond History Center, rounded out our group. Marcus F. King, a longtime and knowledgeable collector of regional antiques who was also a native of the survey area and familiar with its geography and cultural nuances, was selected as our field researcher. Others helped our efforts in specific ways, including Dr. Carole Wahler, who collaborated with us on the particulars of Tennessee pottery. The research effort came to be known as the Cultural Heritage Project, a name that it proudly carries to this day.

Over the next months, Marcus King traveled more than 30,000 miles throughout 15 counties, logging in some 2,800 hours of fieldwork, knocking on doors, following leads, and eventually assembling an impressive archive of photographs, slides, and data sheets on more than 2,000 objects representing each part of the survey area. He kept a daily journal of all his appointments, most of which were fruitful encounters with enthusiastic owners of local artifacts. Everybody he met with seemed to want to feed him before they got down to the business of showing him their heirlooms, and he became familiar with where the best peach cobbler or the strongest coffee could be found, as well as the most unusual ways to make use of local produce. (Only twice was he turned away: the first time shooed off the property by an elderly lady who was distinctly wary of a stranger's arrival, and the second time politely refused a follow-up visit by a skeptical son who clearly thought that the family antiques were about to be compromised.)

Due to the sheer distance Marc had to travel, and the number of documentation visits that were essential to achieving our goal, I assumed the role of photography administrator. Our weekly meetings were crammed full with the transfer of field notes, journal entries, expense vouchers, and the numerous rolls of film to be developed, as well as the contact sheets from the previous weeks, sorted and keyed to the correct documentations. On occasion, when he found a particularly rich site—usually the home of one of the region's early settler families—I would go along for a day of tea drinking, genial visiting, and wonderful documenting.

The largest numbers of objects were found in the counties nearest the old Great Road, a main stage route connecting the eastern seaboard to the western frontiers. Areas farther away were settled sparsely and late, generally yielding fewer items. We found scores of examples of locally made furniture, pottery, and textiles, but fewer examples of less utilitarian artwork, as expected in the frontier environment. Metalwork was well represented by iron products, and the handicrafts of a number of silversmiths and tinsmiths found their way into our records.

By six months into the survey, we became increasingly enthusiastic about what the fieldwork was uncovering, including locally made Chippendale, Federal, and Empire furniture (handcrafted to standards of more urban cabinetmakers anywhere), abundant pottery with distinctive forms and unique decorative embellishments, and beautiful textiles that spoke volumes of family traditions and of natural resources put to useful purposes. By the end of two years, we knew the survey would yield far more than a single summary exhibit, and at the end of a decade it has produced a wealth of resources: a useful archive, a long-running series of exhibitions (fourteen to date) and companion publications, a new permanent collection, and now, this book.

Meant for interested general readers, collectors, museum curators, antique dealers and, indeed, any student of American culture, this volume is essentially a primer, a means to identify the stylistic elements that can be attributed to the handiwork of nineteenth-century artisans working on the Virginia and Tennessee frontier. What the reader will find throughout are telling details—the turn of a cabinet's foot, a particular use of woods, the distinctive shape of pottery—which, taken together, are illustrative of Great Road style.

The introduction provides a general overview of the region and its decorative arts. Each of the chapters that follow focuses on particular artifacts—furniture, chairs, textiles, pottery, painting and decoration, metalwork, baskets, and musical instruments—with illustrations of compelling examples documented through the Cultural Heritage Project, and a list of those artisans who have thus far been identified. The 1850 and 1860 population census records were used to create a reference to the artisan population at midcentury, when occupations were first recorded. The lists are not exhaustive; only those individuals whose principal occupations are relevant appear. The size and inclusiveness of the rosters also reflect the fact that many artisans included in the survey had not begun their local work by 1850–60, and early artisans had died or moved away.

As museum director, it has been my role to oversee the research and curatorial efforts that inform this publication, and in so doing I have gained a new field of interest along the way. I invite you to join me in getting acquainted with the cultural legacy of this region, and to bear witness to the lively style and blend of traditions employed by early artisans as they combined utility with beauty to suit the local market.

Our own research is ongoing, and the rich and varied decorative arts legacy of this region surely calls for additional investigation by others as well. It is our hope that *Great Road Style: The Decorative Arts Legacy of Southwest Virginia and Northeast Tennessee* will form the foundation for this worthwhile and exciting endeavor.

Acknowledgments

Many people deserve warm thanks for their role in initiating and carrying forward the fieldwork and exhibitions, none more so than the project's lead consultant, Roddy Moore, Director of the Blue Ridge Institute at Ferrum College, as well as our project team—Wallace Gusler, former Master Gunsmith, Colonial Williamsburg; Vaughan Webb, Assistant Director, Blue Ridge Insititute; Colleen Callahan, Curator Emeritus of Costume and Textiles, Valentine Richmond History Center—and our field researcher, Marcus F. King. Their scholarship and commitment ensured the integrity of the research, and they continue as colleagues to inform our ongoing efforts. Appreciation is also extended to a regional panel of historians who met with us early on to discuss and provide advice for the fieldwork and project goals, including Charles Bartlett, Janet Blevins, Nell Bundy, Barbara Crawford, Klell Napps, Mack Sturgill, and Ross Weeks.

Realizing that little material was held in public collections, we knew most of the fieldwork would have to focus upon private residences. The individuals who readily welcomed us into their homes to document family heirlooms, and in many cases permitted us to borrow these items for exhibition, deserve special appreciation. They number in the hundreds, and without their enthusiastic participation, none of the research, nor the resulting archive, exhibitions, and book, would have been possible.

Sincere appreciation also goes to Furthermore: a program of the J. M. Kaplan Fund, and to my colleagues at William King Regional Arts Center, its board of trustees and staff, for their support of the Cultural Heritage Project and this publication.

A last and very special thank-you is extended to Mary Belle Price for her generous commitment to all aspects of the Cultural Heritage Project, and especially to this book.

It is thus with deep gratitude and a hearty salute that we thank the individuals and institutions who have supported the fieldwork and those who allowed us to document their objects, thus providing the means to create this lasting and permanent record of the region's cultural identity.

Individual lenders to exhibitions included:

Mr. and Mrs. Bruce Addington
Robert Duff Alexander
Georgia Allen
Ralph and Sarah Arthur
Betty Kreger Atkins
Tom Atkins
Houston Banner Collection
Beverly Quillen Barker
Dorothy Johnson Blom
Bob and Melvene Boone
Joe and JoAnn Booth
Wilson and Lynn Beamer
Mrs. Claiborne W. Beattie Jr.
Mrs. Ora Elena Bonham
Ed Bordett
Mr. and Mrs. George W. T. Bowen

Mr. and Mrs. Rees T. Bowen VI
Mr. and Mrs. Rees T. Bowen VII
Colleen R. Callahan
Howard Campbell
Dr. and Mrs. E. Malcolm Campbell
Mary Jo Case
Joe and Susan Chase
Harriet White Gwathmey Chinn
Dan and Doris Chrisman
Lee Stuart Cochran
Thomas Rosser Cochran Jr.
Gene Robinson Cole
Tom and Rita Copenhaver
Lou Crabtree
Edwin R. Craig III and Jean Craig Keister
Mrs. C. J. Curtis

Mrs. Edwin B. Denton

Lynda and Gaines Dickinson

Richard H. Doughty

Mary Virginia F. Edmonds

Katherine L. Edmondson

Martha Lee Love Edmondson

Ken and Jane Farmer

Sharon Emmert Fletcher

Haskell Fox Jr. and Leon Coker

E. S. Fugate III

E. S. Fugate IV

Mrs. David Greear

Betty Greene

Lucie G. Greever

Jean P. Hale

Mrs. Winfield B. Hale III

James and Melinda Hatfield

Mrs. Caleb Hawkins

David and Alethia Haynes

Kathleen Hedgpeth

Mr. and Mrs. D. G. Heffinger

Gerald and Kitty McConnell Henninger

Charlie Herndon

Goldine Higginbotham

Jim and Louise Hoge

Joyce Holcomb

Ann Kelley Holler

Minnie Minnick Jarrell

Mary B. and Vernon Jenkins

Ben and Merry Jennings

Jo Johnston

Leigh McKeever Jones

Mr. and Mrs. Henry S. Keller

Allene Kelly

Anna Ford Kelly

Jim and Lisa Kelly

Craig Kendrick

David and Nanci King

Marcus and Elinor King

Mrs. Brad Kreger

Alice Wolfe Lanier

Betty Rosenbaum Laningham

Louise B. Leslie

Vicki Lane Marsh

Woodrow McGlothlin

Mr. Charles McKeever

Lena Cantrell McNicholas

Ida McVey

Alma Meadows

Thomas E. Merrihue

Walter Robertson Milborne

Buddy and Jeanie Kreger Mitchell

James Cummings Moore

Pete Moore Antiques

Roddy and Sally Moore

Rufus Morison

Klell and Helen Napps

Billie Pecktal

Peggy Potts

Bob and Marilou Preston

Mrs. Glenn C. Price

James H. Price

Mr. and Mrs. John R. Quillen

Eva C. Prillaman and Wm. Clark
    Descendants

Grace Addington Ratliff

Joy Rhea

Anne Stuart Richardson

David and Betty Ringley

Mrs. Claude L. Roberts

John R. Robinson

Kyle Robinson

Rob Romans

Mrs. Fred Rosenbaum

Steve and Carol Ryan

Ed and Mary Scheier

Flora P. C. DeBusk Scott

Mrs. Dudley Senter

Tony and Marie Shanks

Kathleen White Sheftall

Martha Grant Shipley
Marivene Fox Slemp
Anne Bowen Smith
John Henry and Pat Smith
Mary Virginia S. Smith
Whitley Hayter Smith
Sue Bond Smith
Peggy P. Snapp and Descendants
    of Lawrence Snapp
Martha A. Snyder
David and Nan Spainhour
Ida M. Stacy
A. C. St. Clair Jr.
Kimball Sterling
Mrs. Franklin R. Stewart
Mr. and Mrs. G. R. C. Stuart
Mr. and Mrs. Walter Preston Stuart
Mr. and Mrs. William A. Stuart
Hetty Sutherland (Mrs. E. J.)
Brad Swanson
Father Charles and Evelyn Thayer
Opal Charles Thomas
Ashley McKeever Thomes
Carole Wahler Collection
Mrs. E. H. Warren
Jerry E. Waters
Vaughan Webb
Estate of John Drury Webster
Charles Weisfeld Family
Martha and Robert Weisfeld and the
    Abingdon Virginian newspaper
Cecil Bowen Wendell (Mrs. George E.)
Brenda White
Mr. and Mrs. James Lowry White
Eleanor Jane Wolfe
Emmitt F. Yeary
Monty and Linda Young
Namuni Hale Young

Institutional lenders to exhibitions included:

Blue Ridge Institute and Museum,
    Ferrum College
Brook Hall, Ltd.
Carroll Reece Museum, East Tennessee
    State University
The Currier Gallery of Art
Higginbotham House Museum
Historic Crab Orchard Museum and
    Pioneer Park
Historical Society of Washington County
John Fox Jr. Museum
John Rice Irwin's Museum of Appalachia
Kegley Library, Wytheville Community
    College
Lonesome Pine Arts and Crafts
    Association
Museum of the Confederacy
Rocky Mount Museum
Sinking Spring Presbyterian Church
Smyth County Historical and Museum
    Society
Southwest Virginia Museum and State Park
Special Collections Library, Duke
    University
Tennessee State Museum, Tennessee
    Historical Society Collection
Town of Abingdon
Town of Wytheville Department of
    Museums
The Valentine Museum, Richmond History
    Center
Virginia Department of Historic Resources
Virginia Historical Society
Virginia Museum of Fine Arts, Richmond
Washington County, Va., Courthouse
William King Regional Arts Center,
    Cultural Heritage Collection

Businesses, foundations, and individuals that have provided generous support for the field-work, collection, and exhibitions include:

Bristol Compressors, Inc.
Columbus McKinnon Corporation
The Richard Gwathmey and
    Caroline T. Gwathmey Trust
Highlands Union Bank
King Pharmaceuticals, Inc.
Kiwanis Club of Abingdon
Mr. and Mrs. Edwin F. LeGard
Massengill-DeFriece Foundation, Inc.
National Endowment for the Arts
NationsBank (Bank of America)
Old Abingdon Bed and Breakfast
Mary Belle Price (Mrs. Glenn C.)
The Mary D. B. T. Semans Foundation
The C. Bascom Slemp Foundation
Triad Packaging, Inc.
Virginia Commission for the Arts
Virginia Foundation for the Humanities
Washington County Preservation
    Foundation
Trustees, William King Regional Arts
    Center

Except as noted in the illustration credits (see copyright page), all photographs are by James H. Price, whose skill and attention to detail have ensured that the images included in this book are clear and accurate representations of the cultural heritage of this region.

Introduction

The Great Road (also known as the Great Philadelphia Wagon Road, Great Valley Road, and Great Wagon Road) was a central factor both in the settlement of Southwest Virginia and Northeast Tennessee and in the material culture that developed near it. Other roads branched off the Great Road, some becoming primary arteries themselves, such as the Wilderness Road that carried settlers still farther west through the Cumberland Gap.

The decorative arts/material culture legacy of this region developed against the backdrop of European settlement of the frontier that lay just across the Blue Ridge Mountains from the eastern seaboard colonies. Prior to the middle of the eighteenth century, this mountain range proved a steep and effective barrier to wholesale migration beyond. Only occasional expeditions into the "interior" by explorers and traders gave any clue to the rich timber, roaring rivers, and endless land that stretched out seemingly forever past its nearest peaks.

Silk stockings, 1860, Smyth County, Virginia (see fig. 7)

1

Indian trails traversed the area. Principal among these was the Great Warrior's Path, which ran from the Great Lakes region south through Pennsylvania and Maryland into the Valley of Virginia, where it continued into western Virginia and south to the Carolinas. Eventually, governors of the eastern colonies negotiated treaties with the local American Indian tribes that kept the latter away from the Valley of Virginia, thus opening it up to increased European exploration. As a result, and despite continued and localized stiff resistance from some of the indigenous inhabitants, explorers and a growing number of settlers began to use the Great Warrior's Path in search of opportunities that lay to the west. By the end of the eighteenth century, wars and localized skirmishes between early homesteaders and the native population had ended, and settlement of Virginia's frontier territories proceeded at a rapid pace. (By way of example, the population of Washington County, Virginia, rose from 5,625 in 1790 to 12,156 in 1810.[1])

Transportation was the key to settlement, and much of this was centered along the Great Warrior's Path, which became a main migration route. Gradually, the new travelers gave it new names, and it became known as the Great Philadelphia Wagon Road, the Great Valley Road, or simply the Great Road, as it was called locally in western Virginia. Artisans followed settlers, adding to the population and meeting the market needs of a new frontier economy that soon supplied everything from furniture and pottery to textiles, baskets, guns, and metalwork.

Positioned in the midst of vast stands of timber, rivers and streams, mineral deposits, and a good transportation artery, the emerging regional economy was poised for a prosperity that would continue through the antebellum era. Early towns such as Abingdon, Jonesborough, Greeneville, and Rogersville prospered due to their strategic location along the Great Road. Their citizens enjoyed access to much the same goods as were available elsewhere. Products not made locally were shipped in from the eastern seaboard and other markets. An 1809 inventory of Abingdon's King and Lynn Store, which was located in Washington County, Virginia, lists items that some might be surprised to find this far west at such an early date, including English Queens Ware, delft, violin strings, watch crystals, mirrors, linen handkerchiefs, velvet ribbons, garnet beads, silk neck scarves, and more than twenty-five types of specialty fabrics.[2]

In turn, goods made locally were shipped out, both overland and by river. Markets for local products extended well beyond the region, even at the start of the nineteenth century. A ledger dating to the early 1800s from Brook Hall, a large res-

1. Espenshade, *Potters on the Holston*, 9.

2. *Great Road Style: Decorative Arts of Southwest Virginia, 1780–1860* (WKRAC exhibition guide); Historical Society of Washington County (Virginia), "King and Lynn Inventory" (1978), 14–19.

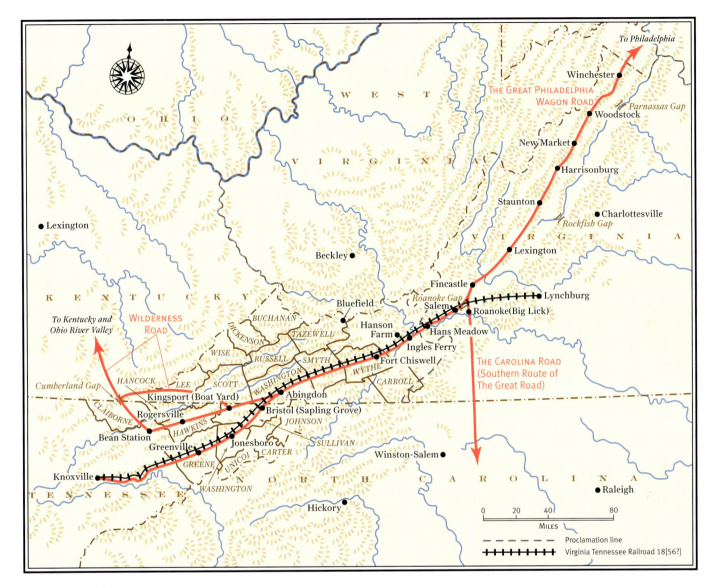

Fig. 1. The Great Road

idence and working farm in Washington County, Virginia, notes freight hauled to Richmond, Baltimore, and Georgia. Saltville, in present-day Smyth County, exported salt.[3] When the water was sufficiently deep, it was possible to float freight on the Holston River from Saltville and the Abingdon area of Virginia to Tennessee and on to the Mississippi River for points south, all the way to New Orleans. The fact that nine boat builders are listed as late as 1850 in the Smyth County population census confirms the existence of a brisk river trade.

3. *Great Road Style: Decorative Arts of Southwest Virginia, 1780–1860* (WKRAC exhibition guide).

Early fortunes were made by enterprising businessmen, who used the area's rich natural resources to their advantage. Colonel James White of Abingdon, a self-made man whose estate was worth $750,000 when he died in 1838, is one example. His wealth came from the lead mines in Wythe County, the saltworks in Smyth County, and various other ventures. It was said that his business interests were so extensive that he could travel all the way from Virginia to Alabama without having to spend a night on property that was not his own.

Even farmsteads showed signs of prosperity. The 1793 probate inventory for potter James Glenn of Washington County, Virginia, included seven horses, one milk cow and twelve other cattle, five sheep, a turning lathe, loom, woolen wheel, spinning wheel, eight plates of Queens Ware, tea ware, pewter plates and platters, a Bible, and seven other books.[4]

Agriculture was central to most settlers' existence. Locally produced merchandise—plows, wheels, hinges, and nails—supported the farmer's livelihood, while artisans produced those things essential to domestic life. Potters, cabinetmakers, tanners, blacksmiths, tinsmiths, silversmiths, chair makers, gunsmiths, and wagon makers all contributed to the local economy and the growing population.

The region flourished throughout the first half of the nineteenth century. The town of Abingdon emerged as a vibrant commercial center, as an 1835 account makes clear:

It is situated on the great valley road, about 8 miles north of the Tennessee boundary, at the southeast side of a mountain ridge, about 7 miles distant from either of the two main forks of the Holston River. . . . Abingdon contains, besides ordinary county buildings, between 150 and 200 dwelling houses, many of them handsome brick buildings. There is an academy for females and one for males, 2 hotels kept in good style, 3 taverns principally used for the accommodation of wagoners, 1 manufacturing flour mill, 9 mercantile houses, some of which are wholesale establishments and sell goods to the amount of one hundred and fifty thousand dollars annually, 3 groceries, 1 woolen and 2 cotton manufactories and one well-established nursery. There are 4 tanyards with saddle and harness manufactories attached to them, 10 blacksmiths' shops, 1 hat manufactory and store, 6 wheelwrights and wagon makers, 2 cabinet warehouses, 3 brick-layers, 2 stone masons, 3 house carpenters, 3 watchmakers and jewelers, 2 boot and shoe factories, 3 house and sign painters, 2 coppersmiths and tin-plate workers and 3 tailors. Population, 1000 persons, of whom thirteen are resident attorneys and 3 regular physicians. As a specimen of the flourishing condition of this town, we must mention that a quarter acre lot, situated near the Courthouse, recently sold for upwards of $4000.[5]

4. Espenshade, *Potters on the Holston*, 54.

5. Summers, *History of Southwest Virginia*, 641–42.

Fig. 3. John Montgomery Preston (1788–1861), who became the first mayor of Abingdon in 1834.

Fig. 4. Formal wool dress, ca. 1830, from the Preston family.

Good transportation continued to be a factor in the region's success. By mid-century, the Great Road was a busy thoroughfare; the Virginia and Tennessee Railroad had been extended from Lynchburg, Virginia, to Abingdon by 1856, and to Knoxville, Tennessee, by a year later. An 1859–63 ledger from Abingdon's H & Co. general store reveals a comprehensive, wide-ranging stock—from chickens, eggs, and mustard to lumber, nails, and escutcheons to linens, boots, and gloves—and gives us a snapshot of a prosperous citizenry whose preferences included exotic foods, fine textiles, ready-made clothing, and decorative items for the home. The ledger pages record purchases of numerous and varied goods: kid

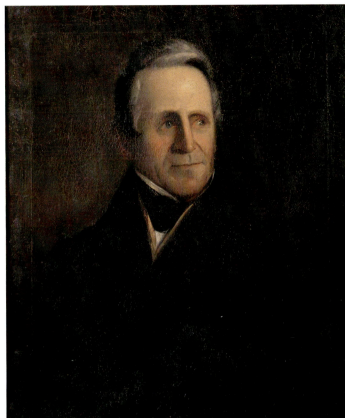

Fig. 6. John Campbell, fifth treasurer of the United States, 1829–39. Also from Abingdon, he was David Campbell's brother.

Fig. 5. David Campbell (1779–1859), thirty-first governor of Virginia, elected in 1837 to succeed his Abingdon neighbor, Governor Wyndam Robertson. John Buchanan Floyd, also from Abingdon, became Virginia's governor in 1849. (The Library of Virginia)

gloves, dress coats, dozens of pairs of hose, a butter knife, linen table cloths, pearl buttons, fine-tooth combs, a gold watch, silk scarves, organdy lawn, violin strings, bottles of whiskey and countless yards of linsey, Irish linen, calico, packaged dyes, and velvet vests, trimming, and ribbons.

The artisan culture that gradually developed in the region responded to two factors: makers and settlers alike arrived with a learned sense of style and preference, and artisans continued to move around, expanding the process of acquiring new styles and techniques. The major groups that settled this frontier were Scotch-Irish, English, and German, and their unique cultural traditions added to the stylistic mix. All of these converging influences eventually evolved into regional characteristics that are now known as Great Road Style—a blend of fashion, tradition, technique, and preferred forms and goods that became the signature of local decorative arts.

GREAT ROAD STYLE

Local artisans—cabinetmakers, potters, metalsmiths—would likely have migrated from the more populated and settled Atlantic coast, perhaps learning their skills in Philadelphia or Baltimore. Some probably stopped and worked for periods of time in various places along the route through the Valley of Virginia, acquiring new techniques and styles, before finally arriving in Southwest Virginia or Northeast Tennessee. Most focused on function rather than decoration, and a great many of the region's early handmade objects were thus undoubtedly plain and utilitarian. Surviving examples of finely crafted pieces have nonetheless been documented that show obvious skill and intentional flourishes of grace and beauty.

With very few exceptions, the first furniture made in the region was in the style of English furniture designer Thomas Chippendale, whose design books were first published in London in the mid-eighteenth century. It took time for this style (and for others) to travel across the Atlantic and reach the frontier; as a result, local examples date from the late eighteenth to the very early nineteenth century. The neoclassical period quickly followed, locally represented by Federal style furniture with clean lines, restrained embellishments, and regular proportions. Local cherry and walnut were preferred by local cabinetmakers, with poplar used as a secondary wood for unseen structural elements. Perhaps the largest group of surviving nineteenth-century furniture in the region was made during the Empire period, from the second quarter of the century to approximately 1860. This style of furniture, also built of local cherry and walnut, included such new furniture forms as the two-piece cupboard and followed the national design trends that favored turned side columns on case pieces, veneers, and larger, often overhanging, top drawers.

Cabinets with pierced-tin panels form a distinctive group within the general furniture forms in the area. This largely rural genre was particularly abundant in the region, reaching its heyday between 1840 and 1860. The tins, whose designs reflected a variety of styles and motifs, were produced in several standard sizes, though we do not know whether they were fashioned by tinsmiths or if the cabinetmaker or someone in his shop made them. Both were possible. The tin business must have been brisk, at least in towns, and it seems plausible that they were simply ordered from shops that already were making all manner of useful items, from coffeepots to lanterns to candle molds. Abingdon's 1850 census lists shops for five tinsmiths: David Sears, James Fullen, John Giles, George Bowers, and David Grim. There is, however, evidence that at least one cabinet shop in Wythe County, Virginia, made tin panels (and supplied them to another business); Roddy Moore notes that the Fleming K. Rich shop listed "sets of safe tins" in its store inventory and filled orders for pierced-tin panels for a cabinetmaker in Tennessee.[6] In addition, the daily ledger of sales for Abingdon's H & Co. notes that in 1859, a regular monthly customer was buying supplies such as a cabinet shop would require, including two dozen escutcheons, glue, sandpaper, turpentine, varnish, a varnish brush, a set of castors, drawer knobs, a mill saw file, and— intriguingly enough—"44 sheets of tin."

Beginning in 1850, area census records noted occupations, giving us some insight into the locally crafted furniture trade. Before that, occupations were not listed, and few cabinetmakers signed their work. To further complicate matters, some craftsmen had other livelihoods and made furniture only as a sideline for family and friends. But by 1850, the census lists a number of Tennessee cabinet-makers—fourteen in Sullivan County, six in Hawkins County, three in Johnson County, four in Washington County, and five in Carter County—and Virginia records twelve cabinetmakers in Washington County, ten in Tazewell County, nine in Smyth County, six in Russell County, and three each in Scott and Lee counties. The 1860 census lists roughly the same total number, but only one cabinetmaker was producing furniture in the same place, clear evidence that artisans moved on and moved around. In some cases, they shifted to nearby communities; John "Carpenter" Thompson, age thirty-eight, is listed in Tazewell County's 1860 census after appearing in Smyth County's 1850 census, while Abram Whisman, who worked in Smyth County in 1850, had moved to Lee County by 1860.

Several cabinetmakers, such as John Ball and Peter Henrize of Russell County, Virginia, appear to have set up their own shops, employing apprentices or rela-tives. In Sullivan County, Tennessee, Jonathan Watson, age forty-one, had four apprentices in 1850, and the John E. Rose family of cabinetmakers operated two shops in Washington County, Virginia. Like many other craftsmen, John Erhart Rose migrated to the region from Pennsylvania; census records tell us he was in

6. Moore, "Wythe County, Virginia, Punched Tin."

Abingdon by the early nineteenth century before moving to the general vicinity of Knoxville, Tennessee, where an 1824 newspaper advertisement describes him as a cabinetmaker, housepainter, paperhanger, gilder, burnisher, and carver.[7] At some point soon after, Rose moved his family back to Abingdon, where his sons ran two shops through most of the nineteenth century. There were other father-and-son operations in nearby counties as well, including that of Uriah Hiatt and his son, Eli, in Lee County, Virginia; Robb Francisco and his son, Charles, in Washington County, Virginia; and Peter Henrize and his son, James, in Russell County, Virginia. In 1860, the census lists the aforementioned John Ball and his son, Hascue, as operating a shop in Russell County; the same John Ball appears as a cabinetmaker in the 1850 census, which notes that son, Hascue, was age five. These records indicate that at midcentury most of the region's cabinetmakers were from Virginia, North Carolina, and Tennessee, while a few others were born in New York, South Carolina, and Pennsylvania. Only one man—Nathaniel Sherman from Washington County, Virginia—listed his occupation as a bedstead maker (as distinguished from a cabinetmaker).

By 1875, factory-made furniture was available in Southwest Virginia and Northeast Tennessee. This is subsequently apparent in the 1884 records for Washington County, Virginia, which tellingly do not include a single cabinet shop, but for the first time list five furniture dealers.

In the days before this change occurred, chair makers were no doubt included in some of the region's cabinet shops. An 1846 paper label from an Abingdon establishment depicts a chair alongside a chest of drawers, suggesting that both were available for purchase there. The fact that each of these professions did other work related to home furnishings, such as painting and paperhanging, also lends credence to this view. Many chairs, however, were likely made by individuals whose trade was specialized, a speculation supported by the census records. In 1850, there were a dozen chair makers working in this part of Southwest Virginia—five in Washington County (Abingdon), one in Tazewell County, one in Russell County, three in Smyth County, and two in Lee County. In Tennessee, there were two chair makers working in Sullivan County, six in Hawkins County, and two in Carter County during the same period. By 1860, the Virginia tallies had shifted, as Scott County gained four, while Smyth County listed one, Lee County two, and Hawkins County none at all. There were, in total, more than forty chair makers noted as working in the region between 1850 and 1860.

7. Beasley, "Tennessee Cabinetmakers and Chairmakers," n.p.

The Windsor chair, with its plank bottom and spindle legs, arms, and backs, was made in many forms here and elsewhere; some were plain side chairs, while others had fancy crest rails or writing arms and storage drawers. Corner chairs were documented in Virginia's Russell and Washington counties, while chairs from Lee County can be identified by double finials atop the back posts. Most pieces were unsigned, although one late-nineteenth-century chair maker working in the area branded his work with his name, "MALONE," in capital letters on a back slat. Virginia's Hawthorne chairs, produced in Washington County from the third quarter of the nineteenth into the early twentieth century, show a distinctive backward splay to the back rails.

Textiles, unlike other forms of historic material culture, were usually made by the family for the family, where many have remained as heirlooms through multiple generations. Itinerant weavers, often men, traveled regularly through rural areas, working to order. For the most part, however, the production of fabric and finished textiles was one of the few crafts largely dominated by women; this contributes to the all-in-the-family nature of cloth, and possibly to its abundant preservation. The vast majority of textiles were undoubtedly plainly made and intended for hard wear, often used and reused to the point of disintegration. Despite this, examples have survived that provide a legacy of women's daily work, from the purely functional to the artistic. Materials produced at home included all manner of bedcovers, towels, sheets, petticoats, dresses, and coats, made from homegrown and -spun linen and wool, and occasionally store-bought cotton.

Perhaps nothing represents the artistic expression of this region's nineteenth-century woman better than the handwoven coverlet. Most were made in the overshot style, dyed indigo blue or madder rose, and woven in patterns using paper drafts as guides. Many survive in pristine condition. Another type of bedcover, similar to the handwoven coverlet but in fact a very different product, was the wool quilt, generally known as a linsey-woolsey or linsey quilt. Combining both weaving and quilting, linsey-woolseys were made of two layers of fabric, either woolen or a combination of wool and linen, and were warm and heavy, well-suited to the cold early winters of Southwest Virginia and Northeast Tennessee. Bed rugs were even more so, and though these are exceptionally rare, one regional example (not shown), dated 1833, has been documented in Tazewell County, Virginia.

There were plenty of local resources from which to make these fabrics, and evidence points to regionwide wool-based textile production. The 1850 agricultural

Fig. 7. Silk stockings, detail, 1860, Smyth County, Virginia
This pair of stockings was hand-knit from silk cultivated and produced at the Sanders family plantation, White Hall, near Chilhowie, Virginia. The stockings have initials and the date, 1860, worked into the tops. The mulberry trees that were used to feed the silk worms were still growing in Smyth County in the early 1920s.

census indicates that there were 98,559 sheep in the Southwest Virginia counties of Russell, Scott, Smyth, Tazewell, and Washington.[8] The population census for 1860 records many weavers—all women—26 of whom were within the town of Abingdon alone, with almost 200 in Scott County. Russell County's census lists such related occupations as spinners and knitters. In 1870, the manufacturers' schedule of Smyth County included a woolen factory, and by 1884 there were three woolen mills as well.[9] There is even evidence of local silk being produced by one Smyth County family, most likely the remnant of a seventeenth-century effort by the Virginia General Assembly to encourage silk making as a statewide industry.[10] Evidence also exists regionwide of flax grown for the production of linen.

Some families created enduring traditions in home textile production, passing down not only the product but skills, techniques, and patterns as well. These families have provided us a cupboardful of keepsakes and afforded us a glimpse into a vanished way of life. Textile production was time-consuming and often required the participation of many hands over a long period, from the growing of flax and the raising of sheep through to the spinning of thread and the weaving of fabric, leading ultimately to the creation of a finished product.

8. *U.S. Agricultural Census.*

9. *U.S. Manufacturer's Census.*

10. McConnell, *Sänders Säga*, 210.

Like woolen coverlets and linsey-woolseys, pieced and appliquéd cotton quilts were found in most homes throughout the nineteenth century. Few of these survive from before the second quarter—most were likely casualties of daily use—but many remain from the second half of the century that attest to a cotton quiltmaking tradition. As in other places, quiltmaking died out as the century ended, only to be revived as a popular craft during the 1920s.

Local pottery production spanned more than a century, waning only when the effects of mass manufacturing and changes in food-storage preferences spelled the end of the market for handmade utility wares. From the fourth quarter of the eighteenth to the last quarter of the nineteenth century, the presence of good local clay and a prospering population enabled area potteries to thrive. Research has uncovered a robust regional tradition near the Great Road, from Wythe through Smyth and Washington counties in Virginia, and on into Sullivan, Carter, and Greene counties in Tennessee. Many potters had a similar cultural heritage—principally German, Scotch-Irish, or English. A number came from Pennsylvania and brought their knowledge of its wares with them, and local traditions were similarly influenced by Moravian pottery from nearby North Carolina. Often, several potters hailed from a single family, and intermarriage between families of potters was not uncommon. These factors, together with the presence of itinerant potters in the region, meant that similar ideas were constantly absorbed and circulated throughout the local industry.

Early potters—those working before mid-nineteenth century—produced earthenware, which had a distinctive orange color due to the high iron content of the local clay, made more pronounced by lead glazing. Rarely did these potters sign their work, and census records offer few clues to their identities. Nonetheless, surviving vessels passed down through generations of area families, as well as the presence of earthenware in estate inventories and manufacturers' census records, and shards that have been uncovered in the region, all confirm the existence of a local earthenware industry. Its forms and the distinctive oxide decoration applied to some pieces give it the name by which it is known today—Great Road Pottery.[11] The earliest known potters included James Glenn, Andrew LaFever, Peter Wolfe, Nathan Lewis, and Adam Miller, all of whom worked in Washington County, Virginia, near Abingdon.[12] In nearby Tennessee, earthenware potters included Leonard Cain in Sullivan County, Frederick Shaffer in Greene County, and John Mathorn and Isaac Hart, who operated a very early earthenware factory in the

11. Moore, "Earthenware Potters," 528.

12. Espenshade, *Potters on the Holston*, 35, 55.

Carter County area of Turkey Town that used four tons of clay annually (according to the 1820 manufacturer's schedule).[13]

The Cain family ran one of the few named earthenware potteries from which signed pieces still exist. Leonard Cain was born in North Carolina in 1782, and started his pottery business around 1840 in Sullivan County, near Blountville (although deed books place him there as early as 1814).[14] Three of his sons—Eli, William, and Abraham—became potters, as did at least two grandsons (Martin, born in 1851, and J. E., born in 1854).

The health risks of lead glaze, coupled with the discovery of nonporous stoneware that could be fired to higher temperatures, led potters to pretty much abandon earthenware production by the middle of the nineteenth century. Most switched to stoneware altogether, although some Northeast Tennessee potters continued to produce some stocks of earthenware as well. One late example that attests to this is a crock from Carter County, Tennessee, bearing the date 1880 (see fig. 123). Local stoneware was gray or brown and usually salt-glazed; most was left undecorated, like earthenware before it. On those pieces that were decorated, the potter generally used cobalt to create floral motifs and other embellishments. Many of the artisans who produced stoneware signed their work, either by stamp or incising, and thus we have a good record of makers.

Through the second half of the century, both the amount of stoneware being produced and the number of potters working increased significantly. At one point, Washington County supported more potters than anywhere else in Virginia, with the next highest number reported in the Shenandoah Valley.[15] Most of the county's potters clustered in the Osceola and Mendota (Alum Wells) areas; a few worked on their own in other locations. The names of those who made stoneware in the area include Mort, Barlow, Gardner, Vestal, Magee, Davis, Miller, Decker, Wooten, Roberts, and Keys; many of these we know from their stamps or inscribed names, or from later census records (1870, 1880, 1890, 1900), wills and deed books, and newspaper advertisements. Some, like Miller and Keys in the Osceola community, had shops that employed multiple potters. Others, like Charles Decker, J. B. Magee, and James H. Davis (who arrived from the northeast at possibly the same time), collaborated on their wares. The 1870 manufacturer's census notes that the largest shop belonged to Jacob Miller, who employed four hands and produced 14,400 gallons of stoneware.[16] In total, over fifty potters were recorded during the history of the trade in Washington County, Virginia,[17] while Northeastern

13. Smith and Rogers, *Survey of Historic Pottery Making*, 32.

14. Ibid., 55.

15. Expenshade, *Potters on the Holston*, figure 18.

16. Ibid., table 7.

17. Ibid., i, ii, iii.

Tennessee was one of three areas in that state that had a high concentration of potters from 1800 to 1900.[18]

From 1870 on, many potteries expanded and consolidated, as existing one- or two-man operations either banded together or added workers. The single potter and small shop was gradually replaced by larger operations better suited to the growing market, and production primarily for local consumption gave way to satisfying demands outside the area. Shops began to supplement their work force with itinerant potters. Some of these landless tradesmen might well have been day laborers simply following the piecework, but others were successful, well-trained potters who apparently chose not to own land or settle anywhere permanently. One example is J. M. Barlow, who moved from pottery to pottery within Washington County, Virginia, creating signature stamps to match different locations. Others moved their entire operation. One who chose to do so was Charles Decker, who, like several other local potters, was born in Germany. After emigrating to the United States, he initially settled in the Pennsylvania area and worked at the Remmey Pottery Factory. By 1870, he had arrived in Washington County, Virginia, where he leased land near Abingdon and collaborated with other potters, including James H. Davis and James B. McGee. Within three years, however, Decker had closed his Virginia pottery and moved his business to Washington County, Tennessee, some thirty miles away. Decker's Tennessee shop was a large operation, and by 1880 employed six people with a capital investment of $1,600. He called it Keystone Pottery, the name he had given to an earlier venture in Pennsylvania, and it continued vigorous production through to the early twentieth century.

Decker's long-lasting success was the exception, not the rule. By 1900, the market for handmade, utilitarian pottery was waning. Those potters who stayed in business tried to accommodate to the change in the traditional market by producing wares for the garden, the cemetery, and the whiskey trade. The art movement offered another business opportunity, albeit a small one, for some of the more creative potters, but when all was said and done their principal role had been to provide functional wares, and that function was being supplanted and redirected. Unable to compete with urban centers and factories, the production of rural handmade pottery for practical use was all but finished by the turn of the century.

Decorative artwork on the frontier was almost exclusively created by itinerant artists, who braved the back roads and mountains of the newly settled territory to

18. Smith and Rogers, *Survey of Historic Pottery Making*, 12, 13.

earn a living. These traveling tradesmen passed anonymously through the area, going from household to household working on commission, primarily producing portraits, but also applying decorative finishes to interior architectural features, creating illuminated family records, and painting an occasional landscape. Existing records offer tantalizing glimpses of artists who may have called this region home. Although Abingdon's 1850 census refers to three "painters"—David Carter, Hiram Dooley, and Samuel Henritze—it is unclear whether they worked on canvases or houses. Dooley in particular was also known to make chairs and furniture. David L. Clark's listing was more definitive; he described himself as a "portrait painter." And Thomas B. Ratliff was the sole painter identified in Tazewell County's 1850 census.

Ten years later, the word "artist" began to appear in Abingdon's census, in the entries for John Ketran, Thomas Johnston, and a third, unnamed man. This same Washington County, Virginia, census lists one twenty-six-year-old male artist in Emory. Records for Northeast Tennessee tell us that several artists were living and working there during the nineteenth century, including William Bateman, Alexander Smalls, and Samuel Shaver, all of whom appear in the Hawkins County 1850 census. The 1860 census for the same locale lists William Painter as an artist, while in Sullivan County three artists or painters—E. O. Rader, William G. Watkins, and Jacob Wolford—plied their trade.

Samuel Shaver, who left behind a large body of well-documented work consisting of over one hundred portraits, was the rare artist who did call the region home. His parents, David and Catherine Shaver, were originally from North Carolina but had settled in the area—initally in Abingdon, and then in Sullivan County, Tennessee (near present-day Kingsport), where their son was born. David's brother (Samuel's uncle) was Michael Shaver, an Abingdon silversmith. Samuel's long and successful career began around 1832 in Hawkins County, Tennessee. Undeniably talented, his initial success as a portrait painter was likely due, in part, to good connections. His father, a justice of the peace, was an influential man, and the younger Shaver married into a prominent family in nearby Rogersville. His wife was Mary Hannah Elizabeth Powel, the daughter of Samuel Powel, congressman and judge. Such family ties no doubt helped secure the early commissions on which he built his reputation. Thirty-four-year-old Shaver listed himself as an artist in the 1850 census, and he appears as "Professor Shaver" (who taught drawing and painting) in an 1851 catalog for the Odd Fellow's Female Institute. He spent twenty years in Hawkins County, developing his artistic skill and his business. After his wife's death in 1856, Shaver moved to Knoxville, where, as a seasoned portrait painter, his career reached its zenith.

Like native wood and clay, metals and ores are an important part of the region's natural resources. The lead mines near Wytheville played a significant role in the area's early economy up through the Civil War, when they became a target for federal troops, and iron ore is found in the region's mountains, so much so that one chain is known as the Iron Mountains. There were a large number of forges and furnaces in present-day Carter and Johnson counties in Tennessee, and place names—Graham's Forge in Virginia, and Furnace Creek and Laurel Bloomery in Tennessee, to name a few—evoke these early industries.

In their everyday lives, early settlers made use of a great many metal items, which the region's numerous artisans were happy to supply. Blacksmiths, tinsmiths, coppersmiths, silversmiths, and gunsmiths, as well as the laborers who worked in the various operations (such as forge hands, iron masters, and hammermen), all appear among the occupations listed in area census records. The border counties of Tennessee, near North Carolina and close to the mountains, were heavily populated with iron-industry workers. Perhaps the most telling record of iron-related occupations and foundries is found in the pages of the 1850 population census of Johnson County, where four men are listed as iron manufacturers, eight as forge tenders, and nineteen as hammermen.

There were a great many blacksmiths working in each county, in big establishments down to the individual farm shop. Scores of utilitarian objects were made or repaired in their forges, from wheels and horseshoes to andirons and hinges, as well as items for household use.

The heaviest concentration of tinsmiths, or "tinners" (as they were called in the 1850 census), was in Washington County, Virginia; in Abingdon alone there were eight listings for either tin- or coppersmiths. Those shops that sold items made of both materials were fittingly identified as tin *and* coppersmiths (as was the case for David Grim, whose 1872 advertisement in the *Abingdon Virginian* offered wares made of tin and copper). These artisans supplied coffeepots, candle molds, roof tins, and other necessary household items.

Few silversmiths appear in the census records. Sullivan County, Tennessee, recorded one silversmith in 1850 and three others in 1860, listing their birthplaces as Mississippi, Pennsylvania, Virginia, and Tennessee. There was also one silversmith—W. Atkinson, age fifty-seven, born in North Carolina—working in Washington County, Tennessee. In Virginia, Smyth County listed two silversmiths in 1860, while Scott County noted one. Records from Abingdon reveal three silver-smiths working in close proximity on Main Street in 1850: Caleb Baugh (age forty-two), Valentine Baugh (seventy-five), and Michael Shaver (also seventy-five, and the uncle of artist Samuel Shaver). Both Valentine Baugh and Michael Shaver had died before the 1860 census, leaving only Caleb Baugh to carry on the trade in Abingdon (although another silversmith, John [?]Rye, was listed at this time in the Emory area of Washington County). It should be noted that Michael Shaver, like many other artisans, did not list the profession for which he is remembered as his occupation. An 1815 advertisement in the *Political Prospect* announces that he is making watch repairs, and by 1850 he is identified as a dentist. In fact, although pieces he made are the only regional examples of local silver discovered to date, Shaver seldom seemed to refer to himself as a silversmith.

Gunsmiths also practiced a trade essential to frontier life, and many of these artisans came to the area early on. John Whitesides is a case in point; he was born in Rockbridge County, Virginia, in 1809, the grandson of a gun- and silversmith and the son of a clock maker. He moved farther southwest around 1830[19] and is included in the Washington County, Virginia, census by 1850, although his name appears as "Whitndy." Washington County's 1860 census identifies him as John M. Whitesides, gunsmith, and the industry schedule for the same year lists his "gun shop." Regional records include a number of other examples. O. A. Grubb worked in Washington County, Virginia, as did Samuel Gobble, who is recorded in Abingdon in 1860. Lee County listed one gunsmith (Samuel Oxford) in 1850, and one (Robert E. Clauson) in 1860. Thomas Barkhimer and his two sons appear in Tazewell County's 1850 census, as does Leonard Dangerfield (who is listed again in 1860), while James Parker Curtis and Fred Sanders made guns in Scott County.

Baskets, handmade items common to most if not all households, were found in every county along the Great Road throughout the nineteenth and well into the twentieth century. Basket making, which rarely appears as an occupation in cen-sus records, made use of materials that were easily found. Local oak, rye, and hon-eysuckle were split, woven, painted, stained, and ultimately fashioned into useful vessels. Few baskets survive from before the mid-nineteenth century, as many were simply used up, their bottoms rotted or their handles broken from years of hard wear. Nevertheless, the fact that contemporary examples, currently made

19. Crawford and Lyle, *Rockbridge County Artists and Artisans*, 140.

and sold as handicrafts, still employ many of the same forms and materials means that one can study early baskets through their twentieth-century approximations.

Traditional music has been the best known of all regional art forms, and the most influential beyond its geographic borders. The Great Road has left its unmistakable imprint on our national identity in such musical styles as ballads, old-time dance tunes, early country music, and bluegrass. Three instruments were primarily, and extensively, used throughout the area: the banjo, which arrived in America with African slaves; the fiddle, which accompanied settlers from several European countries, as well as England, Scotland, and Ireland; and the dulcimer, which was carried along by German and Swiss immigrants.

Not surprisingly, the rich musical traditions that characterized the area during the nineteenth century nurtured a number of instrument makers. These artisans adapted their construction techniques and added their own embellishments to traditional forms. The typical craftsman made instruments either for pleasure or as a sideline of a related profession, such as cabinetmaking; as a result, census records do not identify instrument makers by occupation. Many of their handiworks were made for use by family members (the primary market), and family lore is thus essential in documenting this part of the region's musical and artistic history.

Handmade dulcimers and banjos are found throughout the region, each distinctive in form to its maker. In contrast, locally crafted fiddles dating from the nineteenth century are scarce; none have been documented in recent fieldwork, even though evidence suggesting that they were produced in the region exists. Abingdon's King and Lynn Store stocked fiddle strings as early as 1809, and violin strings are listed in the H & Co. ledger in 1860. There are other equally tantalizing clues: a fiddle included in an 1814 Russell County inventory, a dulcimer which appears in a Washington County estate list in 1831, and the dulcimer-making tools noted in Bland County, just a few miles from the Smyth County line, in 1834. Banjos that were made in the area, which are not as scarce as fiddles, do not appear until after the Civil War. By the late nineteenth century, retailers made available mass-produced musical instruments via catalog sales to anyone with a modest amount of money and a mailing address. Even so, the artisans who created handmade banjos, fiddles, and dulcimers continued to practice their craft, and in so doing maintained the vitality of their traditions along the Great Road down to the present day.[20]

20. Moore, *Great Road Style: Decorative Arts of Southwest Virginia, 1860–1940* (WKRAC exhibition guide).

1 🌿 Furniture

Throughout the history of area cabinetmaking, the wood of choice was cherry or walnut, both found abundantly in the timber forests of Southwest Virginia and Northeast Tennessee, with poplar used as a secondary wood. Cupboards, blanket chests, wardrobes, linen presses, tall case clocks, candle stands, chests of drawers, desks, bedsteads, work tables, safes, chairs, tea tables, sideboards, and dining tables—all were made by the region's local artisans. And although relatively few definite attributions have yet been made between cabinetmakers and their work, each locale's furniture is characterized by unique features.

By the start of the nineteenth century, locally made furniture, both plain and high-style, was available, particularly in those towns bordering the Great Road. For the most part, it is safe to say that whatever was being produced in Philadelphia or Baltimore could also be made in places like Abingdon, Virginia, or Greeneville, Tennessee.

Fig. 8. Tea table, black walnut, 28 x 33 inches, 4th quarter 18th century
History places this early piece (which has a birdcage and a tilt top) in the Damascus area of Washington County, Virginia. The use of black walnut is unusual for that location.

Powhatan Shumak, a Greeneville cabinetmaker from that time, would readily agree. In his 1824 advertisement, he states that he "will be happy to furnish customers with all kinds of cabinet furniture, which shall be made of the best materials, in the most fashionable style, and which for elegance and durability shall not be excelled by any brought from the eastern cities or elsewhere" (Beasley, "Tennessee Cabinetmakers and Chairmakers," n.p.).

EARLY FURNITURE

The earliest examples of locally made furniture date from the late eighteenth century, reflecting the rococo style of English furniture designer, Thomas Chippendale, and emphasizing the neat and plain characteristics of eastern seaboard furniture preferences. One of these pieces is a tea table with birdcage and tilt top (fig. 8) from the Damascus area of Washington County, Virginia. Another is a tall chest of drawers (fig. 9), also from Washington County, that exemplifies local Chippendale characteristics. It features a carved shell, the use of dentil molding, the ogee bracket foot, solid ends, graduated drawers, and stop-fluted quarter columns. The local ogee foot is similarly seen on a walnut chest of drawers from Washington County (fig. 10); this piece has a molded top edge, another local design feature. A cherry corner cupboard from Russell County, Virginia, (fig. 11) is yet another example that boasts double rows of dentil molding (like the high chest pictured in figure 9) under the cornice, but with a plain, rather than ogee, bracket foot.

Dovetail construction was used by local makers; this is evident in a Washington County, Virginia, walnut blanket chest (fig. 12) that is dovetailed the full height of the case, and in a blanket chest of similar construction from Washington County, Tennessee (fig. 13). Inlay, which was seldom used by early area cabinetmakers, was usually confined to escutcheons, with the notable exception of Tennessee furniture from Greene and Washington counties. A Greene County corner cupboard (fig. 15) features the distinctive rope-and-tassel and mariner's point inlay found there. The broken-arch pediment with central finial and cove molding are other characteristics common to Greene County cupboards.

Locally, the Federal period emphasized the styles of two other influential English furniture designers, George Hepplewhite and Thomas Sheraton, which featured straighter lines, tapering legs, the use of inlay, and a generally lighter look. New furniture forms included the slant-top desk with tambour, small one-

or two-drawer stands and work tables, and sideboards. The regional use of the French foot is illustrated by a Washington County, Virginia, chest of drawers (fig. 25), one of several similar Hepplewhite pieces documented in the Bristol area. This chest also shows extensive inlay of light and dark woods. A slant-top desk (fig. 26) with French foot from adjacent Smyth County, Virginia, is another example of Hepplewhite style. It has a tambour compartment, made of alternating light and dark woods, in place of the prospect. A nearly identical desk, with decorative inlay and a tambour compartment, was documented in the Burke's Garden area of Tazewell County, Virginia.

Sheraton furniture was made locally during the first quarter of the nineteenth century. The turned, tapered leg (often with ring turnings) found on many local pieces is evident on both a two-drawer stand from Sullivan County, Tennessee, (fig. 28) and a Russell County, Virginia, doctor's medicine stand (fig. 29).

TRANSITION TO EMPIRE

Local chests of drawers made slightly later than the Federal period offer examples of a transition to the American Empire period. Several identical chests were documented in Abingdon, made in one or the other of two shops operated by the Rose family of cabinetmakers. Each chest features paneled ends and a large top drawer (fig. 31). These design features persisted during the Empire period, with a progression to an overhanging top drawer, the addition of turned side columns, and the use of veneering. The period produced what is possibly the largest surviving group of local furniture, dating to ca. 1830–60. New forms included the regionally popular two-piece cupboard with a typical bottom section of drawers or doors and separate top of glazed or paneled doors. Four good examples (figs. 33–36), from Washington and Tazewell counties in Virginia, illustrate characteristics specific to their locales, including the strong raked cornice with dovetails on Washington County cupboards and the bottle-shaped, half-turned columns common to pieces from Tazewell County.

THE GRAND ERA OF PIERCED-TIN FURNITURE

Furniture with pierced-tin panels was made in such abundance throughout the region from roughly 1840 to 1860 that it forms a subset of furniture in its own right.

Though food safes, destined for the kitchen or back porch, were the most common furniture to which tin panels were applied, decorative tins could also be found in more formal rooms, on two-piece cupboards (fig. 40), corner cupboards (fig. 49), and sideboards (fig. 50).

Tins were either nailed on the front (with nail heads showing) or inserted more discreetly from the back. A common size was 10 x 14 inches, but larger tins (20 x 14 or 28 x 20 inches), often formed by crimping together several of the smaller ones, were also used. Designs were made up of small punched holes, or occasionally small slashes, and motifs included flowers, grapes, urns and compotes, scallops and swags, stars, sunbursts, arches, eagles and other birds, fylfots (four-armed cross or swirling swastika), tobacco leaves, hearts, and a variety of geometric shapes. Most tins were mounted with the rough edge facing out, but occasionally they are found reversed. Some were the intricate work of an obviously skilled artisan, as illustrated by a detail (fig. 37) of one of four panels from a Tazewell County, Virginia, sideboard. Like many tins produced in the region, it was simply given a coat of varnish to prevent rusting. Some examples, by contrast, were painted with colors.

Despite the fact that many tins have been refinished or repainted, enough remain in original condition to provide a good group for detailed study. The Cultural Heritage Project survey found that Virginia tins from Dickenson, Buchanan, Lee, Russell, Smyth, Tazewell, Washington, and Wise counties were usually just varnished or finished with some sort of clear sealer, while in Scott County a few were painted (fig. 40). Conversely, in the Tennessee counties surveyed, most tins were painted, including those from Greene, Hawkins, Sullivan, and Washington counties. Painted tins found in Virginia and Tennessee were either decorated with multiple colors (typically blue, green, mustard, red, and gray) or with one shade, usually of green, red, or blue. The tins on a Scott County, Virginia, sideboard (fig. 38), a Greene County, Tennessee, safe (fig. 54), and a Wythe County corner cupboard (fig. 52) are good examples of original green paint.

Wythe County is on the edge of the Cultural Heritage Project survey area, and its safes and their tins are of such distinction that they deserve particular note. Many were made in the Fleming K. Rich cabinet shop, whose work is well represented by a safe with large multicolored tins (fig. 51) decorated with the typical urn, grapes, and tulip motif painted yellow, green, blue, and gray. Large colorful tins are also found on safes from Northeast Tennessee, in the Warrensburg and Bull's Gap areas of Greene and Hawkins counties. These safes, like those from Wythe County, have large wide cabinets and 28 x 20-inch tins with multicolored paint. The Tennessee tin motif bears a sunburst, Masonic arch, and candle (fig. 55). Two similar safes are known, including one (fig. 56) with identical tins that have at some point been painted turquoise.

Cabinet details, too, were unique to their makers and thus to each locale. For example, the sort of safe (fig. 41) seen most often in Washington County, Virginia, follows a basic 54 x 41-inch cabinet form, with one long top drawer (with doweled pulls) set over two doors, a long straight foot turned from the stile, and twelve 10 x 14-inch varnished tins (three in each door and three in each end panel). Most of these tins feature a scallop or swag design over a central footed urn or compote. The wider cabinet, turned foot treatment, and larger and more elaborate multicolored tins of safes from Northeast Tennessee and Wythe County, Virginia, are decidedly different from those in Washington County. Thus, it is reasonable to say that both cabinet and tin designs are distinct from county to county, but that taken together, they form a regionally identifiable style of pierced-tin furniture.

Local furniture continued to follow national trends through the Victorian period, which was characterized by heavier pieces, often with elaborate curves, carved moldings, and sometimes fanciful embellishments that were added by the cabinetmaker (figs. 58, 61).

Fig. 9. Tall chest of drawers, cherry, 78½ x 39 x 23½ inches, 4th quarter 18th or 1st quarter 19th century

This is a signed piece by Francis Keyes, who like many early artisans stopped for a brief time in the area before moving on. The ogee bracket foot and fluted quarter columns are also evident on the chest of drawers pictured in figure 10.

Fig. 10. Chest of drawers, walnut, 38¼ x 43½ x 22 inches, 4th quarter 18th or 1st quarter 19th century

This is one of several early pieces that have descended through a long-standing Washington County, Virginia, family from the Watauga area. Its drawers are lipped and flanked by fluted quarter columns. The molded edge on the top is a local feature. The right front foot is a replacement. This chest is a good example of local preference for the British-inspired neat and plain style also favored by most eastern seaboard cabinet-makers and their customers.

Fig. 11. Corner cupboard, cherry, 91 x
44¾ x 3¼ inches, 1st quarter 19th century
*The double row of dentil molding below
the cornice relates to the chest of drawers
pictured in figure 9. Waist molding
protrudes 1½ inches above two blind panel
doors with molding on the inner side of the
door frames. This is one of three similar
cupboards found in the Big Moccasin
section of Russell County, Virginia.*

Fig. 12. Blanket chest, walnut, 20 x 41 x 20 inches, 4th quarter 18th or 1st quarter 19th century.

This chest is from the same Washington County, Virginia, family as the piece pictured in figure 10. It has dovetail joints extending the full height of the case, as well as a breadboard top. The interior includes a box for storing small items, such as gloves.

Fig. 13. Blanket chest, walnut, 27¾ x 43½ x 20¾ inches, 1st quarter 19th century

This blanket chest from Washington County, Tennessee, has dovetail joinery similar to that pictured in figure 12, as well as a breadboard top.

Fig. 14. Blanket chest, walnut, 24½ x 44¾
x 17½ inches, 2nd quarter 19th century
*An example of a late use of post and panel
construction, this Lee County, Virginia,
blanket chest may have been made by
a cabinetmaker in the owner's family.
The applied beaded molding around
the central panel, which is beveled in
four directions to form a pyramid effect,
is characteristic of furniture from this
locale. The chest descended through
the Silas Suttle family of Jonesville.*

Fig. 15. Corner cupboard, walnut with dark and light wood inlay, 93¼ x 44 x 3½ inches, 1st quarter 19th century
The scrolled, broken-arch pediment with central finial is typical of Greene County, Tennessee, cupboards. Early examples also feature extensive use of inlay, as in the typical rope-and-tassel and mariner's point or star that adorn this piece (see fig. 16).

Fig. 16. Detail of Greene County corner cupboard inlay (from fig. 15)

Fig. 17. Corner cupboard, walnut with light wood inlay, 87 x 53 inches, 1st quarter 19th century

This Scott County, Virginia, corner cupboard has inlay and applied trim, unusual for that area. Reeded applied columns with conical terminals flank the top and bottom doors, each of which has bull's-eye-centered and notched-corner inlay. This piece is from the Weber City area on the north fork of the Holston River, above Hiltons.

Fig. 18. Server or sideboard, walnut
and yellow pine, 39 x 49 x 22 inches,
1st quarter 19th century
*This piece is attributed to Hawkins
County, Tennessee. Its relatively small size
and scalloped apron make it an unusual
piece for the region.*

Fig. 19. Card table, mahogany, 28 x
38 x 18 (closed) inches, 1st quarter
19th century
*Mahogany was seldom used by early
area cabinetmakers, and few card tables
have been found, making this a distinctive
example. It has poplar and oak as
secondary woods, as well as molded
edges, beaded apron, scissor hinges,
and original castors. It descended through
the Town House in Chilhowie, Smyth
County, Virginia.*

Fig. 20. Candlestand, cherry, 28 x 17½ inches, 2nd quarter 19th century
Candlestands were made throughout the region. This is a typical example with baluster pedestal and snake feet, from Smyth County, Virginia.

Fig. 21. Candlestand, walnut, 25 x 15¼ inches, 2nd quarter 19th century
This candlestand has a birdcage, demonstrating that some cabinetmakers from Greene County, Tennessee, were producing high-style furniture.

Fig. 22. Dressing table, cherry, 42¼ x 36¼ x 19 inches, 2nd quarter 19th century
The top of this Russell County, Virginia, table is cherry, while the apron is highly figured mahogany veneer. It is one of the few dressing tables that have been found in the region.

Fig. 23. Tall case clock, cherry, 106 x 19 x 11 inches, 1st quarter 19th century, movement made by Asa Hopkins of Litchfield, Conn.
The clock case was crafted by an unknown maker in Russell County, Virginia. It features cartouche-string and inverted-fan inlay, as well as an inlaid band of walnut bordered by light wood. The bonnet has four full columns and broken-arch pediment with rosettes. The movement has a painted face decorated with an eagle and a shield with 21 stars.

Fig. 24. Sideboard with clock, cherry with veneer, 87½ x 73¼ x 23½ inches, 2nd quarter 19th century
This unusual late Empire sideboard has a built-in clock. The wooden works are German with automaton figures (marked Herzog); five of these remain of the original seven. The clock face is painted with medieval and mythical scenes, and the middle door serves as pendulum case. Four full-turned columns flank the doors, all heavily veneered with crotch-grained cherry. At least one other nearly identical example is known to exist in the area of Smyth County, Virginia, where this piece was found.

Fig. 25. Chest of drawers, cherry with light and dark wood inlay, 40¾ x 39½ x 20½ inches, 1st quarter 19th century
This formal Federal chest with extensive inlay of light and ebonized woods—one of several with provenance in the Bristol area of Washington County, Virginia—is a good illustration of the local French foot. The brass bull's-eye pulls are copies of the originals.

Fig. 26. Desk with slant top, cherry, 46 x 38 x 20½ inches, 1st quarter 19th century
From Smyth County, Virginia, this Hepplewhite desk with slant top has three pigeonholes and two drawers on each side of a tambour made of alternating woods. It is marked with "GG" on the back of the top right drawer. A related desk was located in Tazewell County.

Fig. 27. Stand with two drawers, maple and curly maple, 28 x 19¾ x 18¾ inches, 2nd quarter 19th century
This table is made of curly maple and has inlaid diamond escutcheons. The turned Sheraton leg has a donut ring turning just above a tapered foot.

Fig. 28. Stand with two drawers, cherry, 28½ x 20½ x 19½ inches,
2nd quarter 19th century
*The Sheraton leg on this Sullivan County, Tennessee, table is typical of the
region, with ring turnings near the top and a tapered foot below two ring turnings.*

Fig. 29. Doctor's medicine table, walnut, 29 x 19 x 19 inches, 2nd quarter
19th century
*The top of this Sheraton work table, which held medicine bottles, swivels
to reveal a partitioned well. The turnings on the Sheraton leg are similar to
those found on several tables in the region (see fig. 28). This piece is from
the Rosedale area of Russell County, Virginia, and relates to six similar tables
in nearby Wythe County.*

Fig. 30. Chest of drawers, cherry, 43 x 41 x 20½ inches, 2nd quarter 19th century
This transitional piece (Sheraton/Empire) is from Northeast Tennessee, possibly Greene County. It has mushroom pulls and a cartouche inlay of cherry crotch-grained veneer on the top two drawer fronts. Local cabinetmakers throughout the region tended to use veneering (usually of this particular type) only on the fronts of furniture and over hardwood (often cherry as well), suggesting that the practice was purely decorative rather than a means to cover inferior wood.

Fig. 31. Chest of drawers, cherry, 47½ x 41 x 18 inches, 2nd quarter 19th century
One of several identical Abingdon chests found in the area, a paper label on the back reads, "Manufactured by G. W. and J. D. Rose, Mar. 24, 1846." This transitional piece has paneled-end construction, a turned front foot with back paddlelike foot, large top drawer, and pulls attached by dowels. The Rose family of cabinetmakers operated in two locations in Abingdon, one on the east end of Main Street, and the other near the present-day municipal building. The shops were operated by the sons of Pennsylvania cabinetmaker, John Erhart Rose, who came to Abingdon prior to 1816, then moved to the Knoxville, Tennessee, area before returning sometime after 1824. Like many other cabinetmakers, Rose was also in the housepainting and paperhanging business.

A notice in the *Knoxville Register* from May of 1824 places John E. Rose "at Mr. John Lonas's shop" and goes on to state that he has "received the latest fashions for Sideboards, Bureaus, Dining and Half-round Tables and cabinet work of every description, and pledges himself that his work shall be executed in a style superior to any in the Western country." John Lonas also advertised that Rose "has painted and papered the most tasty and fashionable houses in Abingdon, Virginia and he is determined to paint better than ever has been done in Knoxville" (Beasley, "Tennessee Cabinetmakers and Chairmakers," n.p.).

Fig. 32. Wardrobe, cherry, 89 x 48½ x 19 inches, 2nd quarter 19th century
The Gothic arched panels, ogee feet with double scroll, and sine-wave molding are local to Abingdon. The cupboard pieces are pegged together, allowing the whole cabinet to be broken down.

Fig. 33. Two-piece cupboard, cherry, 85 x 43 x 20½ inches, 2nd quarter 19th century *The two-piece Empire period cupboard was a favorite in the region. This one is typical of Washington County, Virginia, and has been attributed to the Rose cabinet shop in Abingdon. The turned columns flanking the bottom doors, paneled-end construction, and back paddle foot with front turned foot are similar to those documented on several other pieces.*

Fig. 34. Two-piece cupboard, cherry,
85¼ x 43½ x 21 inches, 2nd quarter
19th century
*The deep cornice set at a thirty-degree
rake with distinctive dovetails below
identify this as a typical Abingdon
cupboard, probably from the same
shop as the piece pictured in figure 33.
The base has one long top drawer with
doweled pulls, another Abingdon cabinet
feature.*

Fig. 35. Two-piece cupboard, cherry with veneer, 90 x 46 x 20¾ inches at base, 13¾ inches at top, 2nd quarter 19th century

The baluster or bottle-shaped half-turned columns on either side of the bottom drawers are characteristic of pieces from Tazewell County, Virginia. The drawers have banded veneer fronts and mushroom pulls. This cupboard is from the Pisgah area.

Fig. 36. Two-piece cupboard, cherry, 88½ x 45 x 20 inches, 3rd quarter 19th century
This two-piece cupboard, found in Tazewell County, is attributed to John Thompson. Born in Tennessee, Thompson's entry in the 1850 population census lists him as a twenty-seven-year-old cabinetmaker in Smyth County, Virginia. By the time of the 1860 census he was working in Tazewell County.

Fig. 37. Detail of pierced-tin panel, 20 x 14 inches, 2nd quarter 19th century
This panel, one of four single tins applied to the doors of a nineteenth-century Tazewell County sideboard, is among the most intricately punched examples documented for the region.

Fig. 38. Sideboard, walnut with secondary poplar, 44½ x 62 x 17½ inches, 2nd quarter 19th century
Original green paint covers the tins of this Scott County, Virginia, sideboard. The punched motif is a fylfot design (cross cramponnee or swirling swastika), which is seen in Scott County and several other areas in the region and most likely reflects the German heritage of many of its settlers. There are two recessed tins on each end panel, and the drawers have inlaid diamond keyhole escutcheons.

Fig. 39. Sideboard, walnut, 48 x 83 x 20
inches with 6-inch gallery, 2nd quarter
19th century
*This Scott County, Virginia, sideboard
with gallery was found in the Yuma
community near the North Fork of
the Holston River. Its large tins have a
repeating pattern of open flowers over
a connecting vine. Sideboards with tin
panels have also been found in Russell
County, Virginia, and in Northeast
Tennessee.*

Fig. 40. Two-piece cupboard, cherry,
82 x 41 x 15½ inches, 2nd quarter
19th century
*The original blue paint, over a century old,
still remains on the large, fyltot motif tins
of this cupboard, which was found in Scott
County, Virginia, between Hiltons and
Moccasin Gap. Each of its end panels is
also covered by a single tin. Two larger
two-piece cupboards with pierced-tin
panels set in three doors have been
found in Scott County.*

Fig. 41. Safe, poplar, 54 x 41 x 17¼ inches, 2nd quarter 19th century

This is an example of a typical Washington County, Virginia, food safe, one of a dozen known. All have twelve nailed-on tins (10 x 14 inches), three on each front door and end panel. Most of the tins are decorated with motifs similar to the one seen here— a footed compote flanked by cone-shaped trees, with a scallop or swag across the top—and are simply varnished. Although the cabinets are nearly all made of poplar, which was usually painted, two were found crafted of cherry. The top drawer on this example has doweled pulls, and the doors have a cock-beaded edge. These safes have been found in the Damascus, Cedarville, and Watauga areas of Washington County, as well as in the town of Abingdon. Recent fieldwork has documented a shaving table, attributed to the Rose cabinet shops in Abingdon, with similar foot and drawer construction (see fig. 60).

Fig. 42. Safe, poplar, 54 x 41 x 17¼ inches, 2nd quarter 19th century

This safe has cabinet characteristics consistent with those pictured in figure 41, but in place of a footed compote motif, the twelve 10 x 14–inch nailed-on tins are embellished with a stylized tree flanked by inward facing commas or tobacco leaves. It descended through an early family in the Watauga area of Washington County, Virginia.

Fig. 43. Safe, poplar, 43 x 40½ x 16¾ inches, 3rd quarter 19th century

Leonidas and Oscar Love, who operated a mill, general store, and cabinet shop in the fittingly named Love's Mill community, produced this Washington County, Virginia, safe, one of several known. This example has large 20 x 14–inch tins nailed to the front of each door and end panel, with a modern molding strip placed around the edges. Their decorative motif— here punched with "O Love" and "1858"— is only seen on this maker's safes. The central design is a corn stalk or "space man" with headdress and a (six-pointed) Star of David where the face should be. One of the figures lacks a crown, a common omission. The plain foot resembles the typical Washington County style but is slimmer and includes a lower taper. The ancestors of the present owner were employed at Love's Mill; this is one of five food safes passed down through the generations of his family.

Fig. 44. Safe, cherry, 51 x 38 x 18 inches, 2nd quarter 19th century
Here, the twelve nailed-on 10 x 14–inch tins feature a motif that differs from others found in Washington County, Virginia. The design is an intricately punched side-facing eagle holding arrows and an olive branch, with "James Robinson 1841" below. Tins with bird motifs are found in several localities (see fig. 49), including Washington County, where James Robinson is buried in the Glade Spring area.

Fig. 45. Detail of tin punched "James Robinson 1841" (from fig. 44)

Fig. 46. Safe, walnut, 48 x 41¼ x 18¾ inches, 3rd quarter 19th century
The tins in this Lee County, Virginia, safe incorporate the date "May 10, 1859." Three of these have been joined in each door and end panel to form one large tin with a repeating motif.

Fig. 47. Safe, cherry, 42 x 41 x 17¼ inches, 4th quarter 19th century
This Buchanan County, Virginia, safe is attributed to MeShack Meadows. Its solid ends have a scalloped bottom, and circular saw marks are visible on the back. The tins are recessed into each door, rather than nailed onto the front.

Fig. 48. Safe, unknown wood (probably bleached cherry, maple, or birch), 55 x 48 x 16½ inches, 2nd quarter 19th century
Each door and end panel of this Wise County, Virginia, safe has two nailed-on tins; the punched motif is a six-petaled open flower within a circle, similar to that on a safe from nearby Buchanan County (see fig. 47).

Fig. 49. Corner cupboard, cherry, 84 x 48 x 17⅛ inches, 2nd quarter 19th century
This cupboard was found in Wise County, Virginia, near the Scott County border. It has two 10 x 14–inch bird-motif tins inserted in each door. Inlaid diamond escutcheons are made of light wood, and the cabinet includes some crotch-grained veneer. It is similar to another corner cupboard with eagle tins from Scott County (not pictured) that is attributed to Hiram Starnes.

Fig. 50. Sideboard, cherry, 54 x 86½ x 17¾ inches, 2nd quarter 19th century
The four doors and each end of this Russell County sideboard each have three 10 x 14–inch tins—eighteen in all. Those in the right center door have been replaced. The motif, characteristic of this locale, is a double ram's head or open tulip.

Fig. 51. Safe, walnut, 46 x 52 x 19 inches, 2nd quarter 19th century
This is a typical Wythe County, Virginia, safe, made by the Fleming K. Rich cabinet shop. Wythe County safes are wider than most in other parts of Southwest Virginia. The large, 28 x 20–inch tins (with an urn, grapes, and tulip motif) still have old yellow, green, blue, and gray paint. The Rich shop kept sets of tins in inventory and sold them to at least one other cabinetmaker, so this piece—cabinet and tins alike—may have been their handiwork.

Fig. 52. Corner cupboard, walnut, 88 x
44 x 18 inches, 2nd quarter 19th century
*The tins on this Wythe County corner
cupboard are decorated with a geometric
diamond pattern, another motif often seen
in that area. The lower doors each have
four tins crimped together to make large
panels, both of which are covered with old
green paint. The upper doors each have
six panes of glass; one is a replacement,
while the others are original.*

Fig. 53. Safe, cherry, 48 x 55½ x 18¾
inches, 2nd quarter 19th century
*The letters "U.S.A." appear across the
middle of each tin in this large safe from
Carter County, Tennessee, with the letter
"S" set at the center of a star. Each tin
measures 14 x 20 inches, with chamfered
dividers between them. Two similar safes
have been found in the Blountville area of
Sullivan County.*

Fig. 54. Safe, walnut, 44 x 43 x 16½ inches, 2nd quarter 19th century
*From Greene County, Tennessee, this safe features an added low gallery,
an element occasionally found on such pieces in the region. The four front
tins are 28 x 20 inches, and the ends have two and one-third tins crimped
together. These are decorated with a hearts and diamonds motif, and their
old green paint is original.*

Fig. 55. Safe, poplar, 46 x 50½ x 17 inches, 2nd quarter 19th century
One of three similar pieces found in the Bull's Gap and Warrensburg areas
of Hawkins and Greene counties in Tennessee, this safe has its original
paint—red combed with black on the case, and red, mustard, blue, and
green on the tins. The tins themselves are large (28 x 20 inches); those in
the doors are made up of four tins crimped together, while three similarly
joined pieces are placed on each end. Their punched motif (which features
sunbursts, urns, candles, and Masonic arch) is typical of safes from this
area of Northeast Tennessee.

Fig. 56. Safe, walnut, 48 x 50½ x 17¾ inches, 2nd quarter 19th century
This is another safe found in the area close to the border of Hawkins and Greene counties in Tennessee. The cabinet is similar in size to the example pictured in figure 55 and has large tins (28 x 20 inches) with the same motif of sunbursts, urns, candles and Masonic arch. Though the case retains its old black color, the turquoise paint applied to the tins is not original.

Fig. 57. Safe, cherry, 49½ x 55½ x 18 inches, 2nd quarter 19th century
The intricate motif on the tins of this Sullivan County, Tennessee, safe is
made up of an urn with a central star and blooming plant with berries or
grapes offset by top corner stars and a geometric design around the edge.
The large crimped-together panels recessed into the doors are alike in size
and design to those from Wythe County, Virginia (see fig. 51). Two tins are
also set in each end; similar examples have been seen on a three-door two-
piece cupboard from Scott County, Virginia, close to Sullivan County.

Fig. 58. Dresser with mirror, 87 x 39 x 17 inches, 3rd or 4th quarter 19th century
Found in the Nickelsville area of Scott County, Virginia, this Victorian dresser has solid-end construction, mushroom pulls, diamond escutcheons, decorative carvings, and a store-bought framed mirror.

Fig. 59. Wig stand, walnut, 74½ x 42 x
18¾ inches, 4th quarter 19th century
*The three front drawers in the base of
this one-piece cupboard have handmade
pulls with back plates and are framed with
applied carved decoration. The piece is
attributed to Bill Plummer, an African
American craftsman skilled as a mechanic,
wood-carver, musical instrument maker,
and cabinetmaker, who lived and worked
in Smyth County (see also figs. 189, 190).*

Fig. 60. Shaving table, walnut, 45¼
x 37½ x 19½ inches (with 24-inch posts),
4th quarter 19th century
*Attributed to the Rose cabinet shop in
Abingdon, this piece is particularly
significant as a possible link between
different Washington County furniture
groups. Details include a straight leg
turned from the stile and doweled drawer
pulls, both of which are found on many
safes from this locale (see fig. 41). The
carving and stippling is attributed to
Mabel Kreger (see fig. 64), and the
table is marked "Jan 21 96."*

Fig. 61. Dog dresser, walnut, 37½ x 34¾
x 15 inches (with 34-inch mirror), 4th
quarter 19th century
The two glove boxes in this piece, which is
from Washington County, Tennessee, have
seated dogs and carved pulls.

Fig. 62. Bed footboard, walnut and curly maple, 48 inches, 4th quarter 19th century
One of two similar pieces attributed to Hiram K. Starnes of Scott County, Virginia, this bed, made of mixed woods with walnut and curly maple accents, has a relief-carved eagle and Eastlake reeding.

Fig. 63. Blanket chest, poplar, 22 x 37¾ x 18 inches, 4th quarter 19th century
This blanket chest, with an inlaid central heart, was made by Hiram K. Starnes from Starnes Bluff, near the Fort Blackmore area of Scott County, Virginia. The applied reeded diagonal trim on either side of the front panel is also found on a cupboard and safe attributed to him.

Fig. 64. Carved bench, walnut, 46 x 54 x 17½ inches, 1st quarter 20th century
This high-backed hand-carved bench has the central figure of a mounted cavalryman set inside a wreath within a circle with "CSA" carved above and "DEO VINDICE" below. Dragons and a man's face framed by scrolls appear on either side; the arms are carved with floral motifs, and the seat has a chain-carved border. This is one of at least two similar benches produced by Mabel Kreger. Kreger, who was from Abingdon and taught woodcarving at the Stonewall Jackson Institute for young women located there, also carved tables, chairs, beds, mantels, mirrors and picture frames, bookcases, and boxes.

CABINETMAKERS

Sources: U.S. Population Census Records, 1850 and 1860; Industry Schedule 1860; and Washington Co., Va., newspaper abstracts (*Abingdon Virginian* 1872; *Democrat* 1855, 1858, 1859; *Political Prospect* 1812, 1815; *Virginia Statesman* 1836). Records include artisan information for the Virginia counties of Buchanan, Dickenson, Lee, Russell, Scott, Smyth, Tazewell, Washington, and Wise, and for the Tennessee counties of Carter, Greene, Hawkins, Johnson, Sullivan, and Washington.

Letter abbreviations following a date refer to the census (e.g., 1850C) or industry schedule (e.g., 1860I).

Aston, John, b. Ireland, age 63, Hawkins Co., Tenn., 1850C

Bailey, Robert, b. Va., age 38, Scott Co., Va., 1860C

Ball, Hascue, b. Va., age 15, "apprentice," Russell Co., Va., 1860C

Ball, John, b. Russell Co., Va., age 27, Russell Co., Va., 1850C; age 37, 1860C

Barnes, Lewis E., b. Pa., age 54, Hawkins Co., Tenn., 1850C

Barnes, William, b. Tenn., age 24 (son of Lewis E.), Hawkins Co., Tenn., 1850C

Beattie, Robert, b. Mass., age 24, Washington Co., Va., 1850C

Bickley, Hiram, b. [?], age 29, Scott Co., Va., 1850C

Bishop, Joseph, b. Va., age 25, Tazewell Co., Va., 1850C

Boyd, Charles D., b. Va., age 41, Russell Co., Va., 1860C

Boyd, Jeremiah, b. Va., age 46, Washington Co., Tenn., 1850C

Boyd, Robert, b. Russell Co., Va., age 28, Russell Co., Va., 1850C

Brown, Alford, b. N.Y., age 32, Scott Co., Va., 1860C

Brown, Samuel; *Political Prospect* notes him as cabinetmaker in 1812

Burdett, Thomas J., b. Va., age 38, Tazewell Co., Va., 1860C

Call, Francis M., b. Va., age 30, Smyth Co., Va., 1860C

Carmack, William, b. Va., age 48, Sullivan Co., Tenn., 1850C

Carson, William, b. Va., age 16, Russell Co., Va., 1860C

Carter, William J., b. Washington Co., Va., age 36, Lee Co., Va., 1860C

Carty, Henry H., b. Tenn., age 25, Johnson Co., Tenn., 1850C

Chamberlain, George W., b. Washington, D.C., age 22, Sullivan Co., Tenn., 1850C

Clark, James, b. Va., age 28, Washington Co., Va., 1850C

Cress, Daniel N., b. Tenn., age 34, Johnson Co., Tenn., 1860C

Cress, John, b. Tenn., age 28, Johnson Co., Tenn., 1860C

Criss, Daniel N., b. Va., age 24, Washington Co., Va., 1850C

Cross [?], Jacob, b. Va., age 28, Washington Co., Tenn., 1850C

Culbertson, Ira[h], b. Va., age 26, Scott Co., Va., 1850C; age 35, 1860C

Curd, Bennett, b. N.C., age 52, Russell Co., Va., 1860C

Daughery, Andrew, b. Tenn., age 29, Russell Co., Va. 1860C

Davis, M.A., b. N.C., age 63, Carter Co., Tenn., 1850C

Dedmore, James, b. Va., age 18, Washington Co. (Abingdon), Va., 1850C; age 37, 1870C

Dickenson, Eli, b. Ashe Co., N.C., age 24, Lee Co., Va., 1860C

DoneWilliam, b. Tenn., age 45, Sullivan Co., Tenn., 1850C

Dunn, Theophiles, age 23, Washington Co. (Abingdon), Va., 1860C

Earnest, Harvey, b. Tenn., age 35, Carter Co., Tenn., 1850C

Epling, Henry, Washington Co., Va., listed as having "cabinet shop," 1860I

Francisco, Charles, b. Va., age 15, "apprentice to Robert Francisco," Washington Co., Va., 1870C

Francisco, Robert, b. Va., age 40, Washington Co., Va., 1870C

Fulividen, Robert, age 19, Washington Co. (Abingdon), Va., 1860C

Galaway, William, b. Tenn., age 30, Sullivan Co., Tenn., 1850C

Galloway, George, age 27, Washington Co. (Abingdon), Va, 1860C; listed as having "cabinet shop" Washington Co., Va., 1860I

Gobble, John, age 35, Washington Co. (Abingdon), Va., 1860C

Goins, Franklin, b. Tenn., age 34, Hawkins Co., Tenn., 1850C

Goldman (or Holdman), John, b. N.C., age 27, Carter Co., Tenn., 1850C

Green, Samuel, b. Va., age 60, Hawkins Co., Tenn., 1860C

Haney, John W., b. Va., age 26, Russell Co., Va., 1860C

Harber, John A., b. Tenn., Sullivan Co., Tenn., 1860C

Hawk, Jonathan, b. Tenn., age 21, Sullivan Co., Tenn., 1850C [? cabinetmaker]

Hawkins, William M., b. N.C., age 28, Smyth Co., Va., 1850C

Henrize, James J., b. Va., age 17, Russell Co., Va., 1860C

Henrize, Peter B., b. Va., age 41, Russell Co., Va., 1860C; listed as chairmaker and painter in Russell Co., Va., 1850C

Hiatt, Eli, b. [?], age 21, "cabinet workman," Lee Co., Va., 1860C

Hiatt, Uriah G., b. Stokes Co., N.C., age 49, Lee Co., Va., 1860C

Hiler, George W., "cabinet shop," Washington Co., Va., 1860I

Hillard, John, age 17, "apprentice to John D. Rose," Washington Co. (Abingdon), Va., 1860C

Honeacre, Henry, b. Va., age 35, Tazewell Co., Va., 1850C

Hoofnagle, Daniel H., b. [?], (father from Pa.) age 36, Smyth Co., Va., 1850C

Huddle, Henry, b. [?], age 27, Lee Co., Va., 1850C

Huffmaster, Joseph, b. Va., age 69, Hawkins Co., Tenn., 1850C; age 78, 1860C

Hunt, James, b. Va., age 70, Johnson Co., Tenn., 1850C

Hyder, Henry, b. Tenn., age 35, Sullivan Co., Tenn., 1860C

Jones, Daniel, b. Va., age 18, Russell Co., Va., 1860C

Jones, Green B., b. Russell Co., Va., age 25, Russell Co., Va., 1850C

Keller, Enock, b. N.C., age 65, Smyth Co., Va., 1860C

Kenaday, Soloman B., b. Va., age 27, Scott Co., Va., 1860C

Killinger, Henry, b. [?], age 17, Smyth Co., Va., 1850C

Kinchion, Elliot, b. N.C., age 54, Johnson Co., Tenn., 1860C

Kiser, John L., b. N.C., age 23, Johnson Co., Tenn. 1860C

Kiser, Phillip M., b. N.C., age 26, Johnson Co., Tenn., 1850C

Lambert, Stephen, b. Ohio, age 20, Tazewell Co., Va., 1850C

Lloyd, John L., b. [?], age 19, Smyth Co., Va., 1850C

Mansfield, John, age 23, Washington Co., Va., 1860C

Marvel, Thomas, b. [?], age 40, Smyth Co., Va., 1850C

Mathena, Isaac, b. Tenn., age 17, apprentice, Sullivan Co., Tenn., 1850C

Mayo, Snider B., b. Va., age 55, Smyth Co., Va., 1860C

McNeel, Augustus, b. Va., age 23, Tazewell Co., Va., 1860C

Miles, James Jr., b. [?], age 37, Lee Co., Va., 1850C

Miller, Isaac, age 20, "apprentice to John D. Rose," Washington Co., Va., 1860C

Minga, George, b. Va., age 28, Sullivan Co., Tenn., 1850C

Morton, William, b. Va., age 37, Tazewell Co., Va., 1860C

Neal, James W., b. Va., age 39, Tazewell Co., Va., 1860C

Neel, Robert M., b. Va., age 30, Tazewell Co., Va., 1860C

Niece, Jonathan, b. N.C., age 49, Sullivan Co., Tenn., 1850C

Oaks, Rice, b. Va., age 65, Hawkins Co., Tenn., 1860C

Pallan, John S., Sr., b. Pa., Sullivan Co., Tenn., 1860C

Peoples, Canada, b. Tenn., age 24, Carter Co., Tenn., 1850C

Perkins, Harvey, b. Grayson Co., Va., age 25, Russell Co., Va., 1850C

Powell, Gaston, b. Tenn., age 25, Sullivan Co., Tenn., 1850C

Pruner, William M., b. Ohio, age 34, Smyth Co., Va. 1850C

Quillen, James M., b. Va., age 25, Scott Co., Va., 1850C; age 35, 1860C

Reed, Dudley B., b. Md., age 53, Washington Co., Tenn., 1850C

Reeder, [?], b. Va., age 25, Smyth Co., Va., 1860C

Renshaw, Hosea, b. N.C., age 49, Washington Co., Tenn., 1850C

Repass, William, b. Va., age 34, Scott Co., Va., 1860C

Rogers, Gilbert, b. Va., age 47, Tazewell Co., Va., 1850C

Rogers, Thomas, b. Tenn., age 27, Sullivan Co., Tenn., 1850C

Rose, Andrew, b. Va., age 20, Washington Co., Va., 1850C

Rose, George Washington, b. Va., age 32, Washington Co., Va., 1850C

Rose, Jackson M., b. Va., age 25, Washington Co. (Abingdon), Va., 1850C; age 33, refers to himself as "master cabinetmaker," 1860C; listed as having "cabinet shop," 1860I; age 45, 1870C (refers to birthplace as Tenn.); 1855 *Democrat* reported he had moved his cabinet shop to his residence next to Temperance Hall because other had burned; 1872 *Abingdon Virginian* reported two shops, one in east end of town opposite Academy of Visitation, the other opposite Martha Washington College

Rose, John, b. Va., age 30, Washington Co. (Abingdon) Va., 1850C; age 41, Washington Co., Va., 1860C

Ross, Reuben, b. N.C., age 55, Johnson Co., Tenn., 1860C

Saul, Samuel, b. Va., age 28, Tazewell Co., Va., 1850C; age 38, Lee Co., Va. 1860C

Seabolt, William S., b. Va., age 30, Tazewell Co., Va., 1850C

Seagle, James F., b. [?], age 22, Smyth Co., Va., 1850C

Seaver, John, b. Va., age 32, Scott Co., Va., 1860C

Sheffey, D. M., b. Va., age 28, Hawkins Co., Tenn., 1860C

Shother, John B., b. S.C., age 23, Smyth Co., Va., 1850C

Shupe, John A., b. Tenn., age 23, Johnson Co., Tenn., 1860C

Sipes, Jessee, b. Pa., age 42, Lee Co., Va., 1860C

Smith, Courtney, b. [?], age 45, Scott Co., Va., 1850C

Smith, Henry, b. Va., age 75, Tazewell Co., Va., 1850C

Spurier, William, Washington Co., Va., "cabinet shop," 1860I

Stanfield, James, b. Va., age 38, Washington Co., Va., 1850C

Stratton, William R., b. Va., age 33, Tazewell Co., Va., 1860C

Suiter, John, b. Va., age 52, Tazewell Co., Va., 1860C

Suthers, John H., b. Va., age 43, Tazewell Co., Va., 1850C

S[?]utton, John, b. N.C., age 38, Washington Co., Tenn., 1850C

Thompson, John, b. Tenn., age 27, Smyth Co., Va., 1850C; John "Carpenter" Thompson, age 38, Tazewell Co., Va., 1860C

Thompson, P. J., b. Va., age 40, Tazewell Co., Va., 1850C

Tilson, Henry, b. Tenn., age 36, Hawkins Co., Tenn., 1850C; age 42, 1860C

VanPelt, Alex, b. Washington Co., Va., age 19, Russell Co., Va., 1850C

VanPi[e]lt, A. J., b. Va., age 33, Tazewell Co., Va., 1850C; age 44, 1860C (VanPelt)

Varner, Tinsley, b. Rockingham Co., N.C., age 35, 1850C

Vermillion, Charles B., b. Smyth Co., Va., age 32, Russell Co., Va., 1850C

Watson, Jacob, b. Tenn., age 34, Washington Co., Tenn., 1850C

Watson, Jacob, b. Tenn., age 17, apprentice, Sullivan Co., Tenn., 1850C

Watson, Jonathan, b. Tenn., age 41, Sullivan Co., Tenn., 1850C

Whisman, Abram, b. Va., age 32, Smyth Co., Va., 1850C; age 43, Lee Co., Va. 1860C

Wilcox, Daniel, b. N.C., age 24, Carter Co., Tenn., 1850C

Wilson, George, age 40, Washington Co. (Abingdon), Va., 1860C

Woods, Richard, b. N.C., age 23, Lee Co., Va., 1850C

Young, James, b. Va., age 18, Washington Co., Va., 1850C

Young, James, b. Va., age 35, Scott Co., Va., 1860C

Young, Joseph E., b. Va., age 22, Washington Co., Va., 1850C

[?], David, b. S.C., age 26, Smyth Co., Va., 1860C

[?], Joseph A., b. Va., age 27, Smyth Co., Va., 1860C

BEDSTEAD MAKER

Sherman, Nathaniel E., b. Va., age 50, Washington Co., Va., 1850C

2 ✺ Chairs

Hiram Dooley was perhaps typical of the chair makers working in nineteenth-century Southwest Virginia and Northeast Tennessee. He produced a variety of products, moved around from place to place and in and out of partnerships, and sometimes did not identify himself as a chair maker at all. In 1840, he *was* known as a chair maker and painter in Jonesborough, Tennessee; a notice that appeared that year in the *Nashville Whig* announces that "he has commenced the manufacture of Windsor chairs" and "is prepared to do all manner of house and sign painting, with neatness and dispatch. He will take in exchange for work Iron and Nails. His shop may be found in the west end of town" (Beasley, "Tennessee Cabinetmakers and Chairmakers," n.p.). Mr. Dooley moved by 1850, and is subsequently listed in the Washington County, Virginia, population census. An 1854 advertisement in the *Abingdon Virginian* states that he and "James R. Dedmore, cabinetmaker, are two doors east of Mr. Greenway's Store, Abingdon, Virginia." By 1858, Hiram

79

Dooley had seemingly added cabinetmaking to his skills; the *Democrat* advertised that he had located his cabinetmaking business for "Windsor and Spring Back Split Bottom Chairs, 1½ miles south of Abingdon." There is no mention of Mr. Dedmore by this time (Newspaper abstracts, *Abingdon Virginian*). In a final telling detail, an entry in the records of Abingdon's H & Co. general store from July 1860 notes that H. S. Dooley purchased half a gallon of linseed oil. Yet despite his professed talents as a chair maker—and possibly cabinetmaker—in the 1840, 1854, and 1858 advertisements, Hiram Dooley simply listed himself as a "painter" in the 1850 Abingdon census.

CHAIRS OF ALL KINDS

All sorts of chairs—arm, side, rocking, corner, and children's, as well as settles and settees—were made in the region from the end of the eighteenth through the second quarter of the twentieth century. A late-eighteenth-century Brewster-type arm chair (fig. 65) and a rocking chair (fig. 66) are most likely the oldest chairs documented from the region. Both come from Washington County, Virginia.

The Windsor chair, made in abundance in various forms, is found throughout the region. The local style was the simple plank-bottom side chair with spindle back, straight crest rail, and doweled-in splayed legs, as illustrated by a Washington County, Virginia, example (fig. 67). In Tennessee, its fancier counterpart sometimes had a double crest rail and shaped inserts (fig. 68). Several writing-arm Windsor chairs have been documented, including two in Tazewell County, Virginia (see figure 69 for one of these), and another three in Washington County, Virginia.

Chairs often display characteristics common to one particular area, or that relate to examples from nearby communities. A writing-arm chair (not a Windsor) from Greene County, Tennessee (fig. 70) has back slats and acorn finials that relate to a side chair (fig. 76) from adjacent Washington County, Tennessee. Double finials on the back posts are an identifiable feature of Lee County, Virginia, side chairs (fig. 72). Corner chairs with double backs were found both in Russell (fig. 73) and adjacent Washington County, Virginia (figs. 74 and 75). Chair makers seldom signed their work, with the exception of one late craftsman who branded his with "MALONE" on a back slat (fig. 77).

Fig. 66. Rocking chair, walnut, 43¼ x 17 inches, 4th quarter 18th century
Lieutenant Thomas Tate, a veteran of the Revolutionary War from Washington County, Virginia, owned this chair, an example of pegged construction. The rockers may have been an addition.

Fig. 67. Windsor side chair, painted wood, 32 inches, 2nd quarter 19th century
This simple plank-bottom side chair, one of a pair from Washington County, Virginia, is the most common type of Windsor found in the area. The olive green paint is probably original.

Fig. 68. Windsor arm chair, painted wood, 35 x 21 x 18 inches, 2nd quarter 19th century
The center spindle with a shield-shaped feature and the turned double crest rail with shaped central insert make this a fancy version of the usual Windsor chair (see fig. 67). Though this piece from Johnson County, Tennessee, is missing the front stretcher, the traces of old blue paint are probably original.

Fig. 69. Writing-arm Windsor chair, poplar, hickory, and oak, 35 x 37 (with table top extended) x 19 inches, 2nd quarter 19th century

This is one of two similar writing-arm Windsor chairs found in Tazewell County, Virginia. The drop-leaf writing surface, which substantially increases the chair's size when extended, has double drawers below; these, together with the drawer under the seat, make this a serviceable desk. At least three other examples have been documented from the area—two from Washington County, Virginia, as well as another of uncertain provenance that relates to them.

Fig. 70. Writing-arm chair, maple and hickory, 46½ x 29¼ inches, 2nd quarter 19th century

The recessed ring turnings on the front leg, acorn finials, and four shaped and graduated back slats of this Greene County writing-arm chair relate to a side chair from adjacent Washington County, Tennessee (see fig. 76). The original seat has been replaced.

Fig. 71. Rocking chair, oak, maple, and ash, 45 x 19 inches, 2nd quarter 19th century
Attributed to Washington County, Tennessee, this chair has distinctive canoe-shaped rockers; the small acorn finials on the back posts are similar to those pictured in figures 70 and 76.

Fig. 72. Arm chair, maple, oak, and hickory, 42 x 20 x 15 inches (14½ inches high at seat), 1st or 2nd quarter 19th century
The double finials on the back posts of this piece are characteristic of Lee County chairs; the front posts have ring turnings above the seat, which is woven hickory.

Fig. 73. Corner chair, mixed woods, 32 x 14¾ inches, 1st quarter 19th century
This corner chair, from the Rosedale area of Russell County, Virginia, is one of a set of four probably made on the family property. All have woven river-cane bottoms. The splayed chamfered back posts are similar to those found on examples from adjacent Washington County, Virginia (see figs. 74, 75). The green paint is not original.

Fig. 74. Corner chair, mixed woods, 34½ x 16 inches, 2nd or 3rd quarter 19th century
The slight chamfering above the seat achieves a very minimal splay on this chair, which is attributed to the Wyndale area of Washington County, Virginia. The plain turned legs have one ring turning just above the tapered foot; the green paint is not original.

Fig. 75. Corner chair, maple and hickory, 34½ x 16 inches, 2nd or 3rd quarter 19th century
This corner chair, found in the King's Mountain area of Abingdon, has a woven rawhide seat and slightly splayed back posts which resemble those pictured in figure 74.

Fig. 76. Side chair, maple and oak, 37½ inches, 3rd quarter 19th century
The acorn finials, turned front posts, and three graduated and shaped crest rails relate this chair to the one pictured in figure 70. Note the deep ring turning just below the seat and another above the foot on the front posts. This example, from Washington County, Tennessee, has traces of original blue paint and the original woven split-oak seat.

Fig. 77. Side chair, maple and oak, 36½ x 16½ inches, 4th quarter 19th or 1st quarter 20th century
This is one of several side and rocking chairs known from a family of craftsmen in the Reedy Creek area near Bristol, Virginia, on Gate City Highway. The wide graduated back slats are distinctive to the chair maker, who usually branded the bottom slat with his name, "MALONE." The top rail is pegged twice on each side.

Fig. 78. Side chair, possibly ash, 35 x 13½ inches, 1st or 2nd quarter 20th century
The graduated, curved, and splayed back slats and the ring turning just above the seat are common to Hawthorne chairs, which were made in the Meadowview area of Washington County, Virginia, from the third quarter of the nineteenth through the early twentieth century. This example has one stretcher in front and two on each side, a characteristic arrangement.

Fig. 79. Side chair, hickory and oak, 35¼ x 19 inches, 1st quarter 20th century
One of a set of four chairs made by Jake Kestner of Washington County, Virginia, this piece has splayed back posts like those found on Hawthorne chairs, and an original woven hickory seat.

Fig. 80. Child's paint-decorated rocking chair, unknown wood, 17 inches, 2nd quarter 19th century
This early child's chair has canoe rockers and a wide crest rail, and is decorated with painted country scenes. The back posts have triple ring turnings near the top, and the seat is a plank bottom. The inscription reads "Made for [?] age 3, 1846."

Fig. 81. Child's high chair, maple and oak, 34 x 12 inches, 3rd quarter 19th century
The front and back posts of this Smyth County high chair have ring turnings above the original split-oak seat. The slight chamfer above the bottom rail creates minimal splay to the back rails.

Fig. 82. Child's arm chair, unknown wood, 18 x 12 inches, 4th quarter 19th century

Fig. 83. Child's rocking chair, 22 x 14 inches, 4th quarter 19th century
Both of these pieces have egg-shaped finials and graduated back slats, with hourglass turnings on their front posts (above the seat). The chair, covered by a layer of old lime green over older dark green paint, has a woven replacement seat; the rocker, with its original seat, has old gray-blue paint. Both are attributed to a Mr. Melton, who may have made them for members of his Lee County, Virginia, family.

Fig. 84. Settle or deacon's bench, painted wood, 33½ x 84 x 18½
inches, 2nd quarter 19th century
*This example, typical of settles made in the region, is original to Elk
Garden, in Russell County, Virginia. Individual stretchers connect each
section of the bench, and the back is supported by three 9½-inch-wide
slats.*

Sources: U.S. Population Census Records, 1850 and 1860; Industry Schedule 1860; and Washington Co., Va., newspaper abstracts (*Abingdon Virginian* 1872; *Democrat* 1855, 1858, 1859; *Political Prospect* 1812, 1815; *Virginia Statesman* 1836). Records include artisan information for the Virginia counties of Buchanan, Dickenson, Lee, Russell, Scott, Smyth, Tazewell, Washington, and Wise, and for the Tennessee counties of Carter, Greene, Hawkins, Johnson, Sullivan, and Washington.

Letter abbreviations following a date refer to the census (e.g., 1850C) or industry schedule (e.g., 1860I).

Abst, Abraham, b. Tenn., age 41, Hawkins Co., Tenn., 1850C

Adkins, John, b. N.C., age 62, Hawkins Co., Tenn., 1850C

Blankinbeckler, Calvin, b. Tenn., age 40, Scott Co., Va., 1860C

Booth, Alfred, b. Va., age 42, Tazewell Co., Va., 1850C

Booth, Alfred, b. Va., age 22, Russell Co., Va., 1860C

Boyd, William, b. Va., age 65, Hawkins Co., Tenn., 1850C

Casender, James, b. S.C., age 49, Hawkins Co., Tenn., 1850C

Chapman, William, b. N.C., age 31, Smyth Co., Va., 1850C

Coal, Henry, b. [?], age 37, Lee Co., Va., 1860C

Collins, [?], b. Tenn., age 34, Washington Co., Tenn., 1850C

Dooley, Hiram; in 1858, the *Democrat* advertised his "cabinetmaking business for Windsor and Spring Back Split Bottom Chairs, 1½ miles south of Abingdon"; in 1850 census for Washington Co., Va., Hiram Dooley lists his occupation as a "painter"

Gill, Joseph, b. Va., age 62, Washington Co., Va., 1850C

Goins, Elijah, b. [?], age 63, Lee Co., Va., 1860C

Good, Francis, b. Va., age 30, Scott Co., Va., 1860C

Good, Thomas, b. N.C., age 57, Scott Co., Va., 1860C

Grant, Archibald, b. Mass., age 38, Washington Co., Va., 1850C

Henritze, Peter, b. Washington Co., Va., age 32; also listed as "painter," Russell Co., Va., 1850C; listed as cabinetmaker (and training son James, age 17), Russell Co., Va., 1860C

Herd, David, b. Tenn., age 24, Lee Co., Va., 1850C

Joiner, Mills N., b. [?], age 53, Lee Co., Va., 1860C

Lam, Joseph, b. N.C., age 100, Hawkins Co., Tenn., 1850C

Lane, John, b. Va., age 46, Scott Co., Va., 1860C

Lunsford, John, b. [?], age 39, Smyth Co., Va., 1850C

McCullum, William, age 50, Washington Co. (Abingdon), Va., 1850C

Miller, John L., b. Va., age 40, Washington Co., Va., 1850C

Mills, Thomas, b. Tenn., age 52, Sullivan Co., Tenn, 1860C

Minnick, Jacob, b. [?], age 63, Russell Co., Va., 1860C

Mitchell, John, b. N.C., age 22, Sullivan Co., Tenn., 1850C

Moore, William, b. Va., age 63, Tazewell Co., Va., 1860C

Nelms, Abraham, b. Tenn., age 26, Sullivan Co., Tenn., 1860C

Reed, Robert, b. Va., age 66, Washington Co., Tenn., 1850C

Renshaw, Patrick, b. Va., age 35, Sullivan Co., Tenn., 1850C

Roberts, David, b. Tenn., age 31, Sullivan Co., Tenn., 1860C

Roberts, King, b. Tenn., age 39, Hawkins Co., Tenn., 1850C

Ross, Joshua, b. [?], age 41, Smyth Co., Va., 1850C

Sapman, William, b. Va., age 42, Smyth Co., Va., 1860C

Smith, Thomas, b. [?], age 46, Lee Co., Va., 1850C

South, Steven, b. Va., age 36, Sullivan Co., Va., 1860C

Sturgeon, Arthur, b. Va., age 46, Russell Co., Va., 1860C

Vials, James, b. Tenn., age 66, Carter Co., Tenn., 1850C

Woods, James, b. N.C., age 25, Carter Co., Tenn., 1850C

[?], John, b. Va., age 40, Smyth Co., Va., 1860C

3   Textiles

For people along the Great Road, especially the families who lived in towns, there were alternatives to homespun. Finished textiles and cloth, or the materials needed to create them, were available on the Virginia and Tennessee frontier earlier than is commonly imagined. In 1809, Abingdon's King and Lynn Store carried twenty-five types of specialty fabrics. The railroad arrived in Abingdon in 1856, bringing with it even greater access to products; this is made evident in the 1859–63 inventory of another local store, H & Co., which sold cottons, cambrics, calicos, Irish linens, ginghams, lawns, organdies, linseys, jaconets, muslins, and flannels, in addition to notions such as thread, buttons, and various trimmings.

Detail of cotton pieced quilt
(see fig. 95)

Nonetheless, home textile production seemed to be a part of daily life for most families, those living in town as well as those out in the country, regardless of whether they called a cottage or large dwelling home. To be sure, the nineteenth-century homemaker who resided in remote areas needed to be more self-reliant than her counterpart in town. Contemporary family histories and the abundance of such surviving equipment as old barn looms attest to the fact that most people wove, spun, dyed, knittted, and sewed at least part of what they needed for clothing and the home. Many also raised sheep for wool and grew flax for linen. Some families created strong textile traditions, passing down not only the products but the skills, techniques, and patterns needed to create them. While much cloth was made for purely utilitarian purposes, meant clearly for hard use, some materials were lightly used and stored away as heirlooms. Woven coverlets, linsey quilts, pieced and appliquéd cotton quilts, show quilts, and all sorts of sheets, towels, and clothing—these speak of the region's rich textile history.

Despite the presence of itinerant weavers and the availability of store-bought goods, existing records and oral tradition suggest that many women chose, and indeed preferred, to continue the practice of home weaving. Chilly winters called for warm fabrics, and the housewife turned to what was at hand—sheep and flax—to create her own wool and linen. The processes required knowledge of natural or packaged dyes and proficiency in the use of a broad range of equipment—looms, spinning wheels, warping boards, wool carders, hatchels (heckle, hackle), winders, and scutching knives. There is a particularly strong tradition of handwoven wool coverlets throughout the region, and many good examples date from the third and fourth quarters of the nineteenth century. We know that coverlets were made much earlier, but the profusion of such later examples stems perhaps from both their heavy use and the effects of the Civil War, which disrupted the transportation system that brought in goods and generally caused a faltering economy, and with it a need for self-sufficiency at home. Census records from that time note a significant rise in the numbers of weavers and spinners, primarily women, beginning in 1860. Whether this was due to an actual increase or occurred because women simply began to record home weaving as an occupation is uncertain.

THE HANDWOVEN COVERLET

It is the handwoven coverlet that perhaps best represents the artistic expression of this region's nineteenth-century women. Coverlets were made of local wool, which was dyed and spun and then combined with either homegrown and processed linen fibers or store-bought cotton thread. The spinning wheel and loom were central to the process. Two types of wheels were used—a great wheel (otherwise known as a high or walking wheel) for spinning wool and a smaller flax wheel for processing linen fibers. The loom was large (it was often called a barn loom), and was the final staging site for production. Made from logs, it was situated in the house, where it took up much of a room, or in the basement or an outbuilding. Its warp threads—those running out from and perpendicular to the weaver—were generally made of strong natural-colored fibers from locally grown flax plants. Gathered, allowed to weather, soaked, beaten to break and then stripped of the husk, the flax was at length spun into thread on the flax wheel. Although cotton was rarely grown locally, it was available for purchase in the form of thread, and many weavers used it as the warp, as it was an easy replacement given the time-consuming process of making linen threads. The coverlet's pattern and color came from the dyed wool weft threads, which the weaver carried back and forth across the warp on a wooden shuttle. Most used an overshot weave, in which several of the colored weft threads skip over some of the warp, floating loose and creating a characteristic overshot appearance. Area coverlets usually were shades of red or blue (figs. 85, 86) with some greens. On occasion other color schemes were used, as seen in a black-and-white double-weave coverlet from Washington County, Virginia (fig. 91).

QUILTS OF LINSEY, COTTON, VELVET, AND SILK

The same equipment and natural resources used to make coverlets figured in the production of another local bedcover, the linsey-woolsey quilt. Linsey-woolseys, sometimes just called linseys, combined both weaving and quilting. They were created from two layers of woolen fabric, or a combination of wool and linen, produced by the home weaver on her loom. After placing batting between, she quilted the two layers together, making the warmest of covers. The linsey top could be pieces of this heavy, warm (and scratchy) fabric, sewn together in blocks or strips or solid lengths of seamed pieces (figs. 92, 93).

Cotton quilts, either pieced or appliquéd, were not as warm or durable as their woolen counterparts. Although they were found in most homes throughout the nineteenth century, not many that date to before the second quarter survive, as most were casualties of daily use. Like cotton quilts found elsewhere, Great Road examples often had tops that were pieced or appliquéd using common quilting patterns. At times only the names varied; the local pattern called "Wreath of Roses" that appears on a Lee County quilt is no doubt known by different names in other areas both within and beyond Southwest Virginia and Northeast Tennessee. This particular quilt (fig. 96), still in the family of its maker, Sarah Henderson Russell Evans, has a homespun bottom, like others in the region.

Show quilts, which were primarily crazy quilts, were made in the region during the last quarter of the nineteenth century. Many examples exist of these colorful coverlets, pieced together in a seemingly random pattern. Intended for display rather than for actual use on a bed, some were made of cottons, wools, and flannels, such as one created in 1890 by Annie L. McGlothlin (fig. 100). Others incorporated fabrics cut from suits discarded by the quilters' husbands. Still others, particularly those from the 1880s (when the crazy quilt first became popular), were quite elegant, boasting velvets and silks (figs. 101–103) and featuring varied embroidery stitches. Most were left with no backing, and none were actually quilted.

By the end of the century, home production of textiles for serious use was declining along the Great Road as it was across the country; it would enjoy a revival as a fashionable craft and pastime by 1920, in new quilts with names like "Double Wedding Ring" (fig. 104) and "Log Cabin" (fig. 105).

Fig. 85. Woven overshot coverlet, wool, cotton, and homespun linen, "Sea Star" or "Pine Cone Bloom" pattern, 99 x 87 inches, 3rd quarter 19th century

Rebecca Cecil Thompson Ward (1838–92) is typical of the homemaker/weavers who lived in nineteenth-century Southwest Virginia. She and her husband married in 1855, and their families were among the region's earliest settlers. Like many women of the landed class, she produced her own textiles for home use; surviving examples of her work, including this indigo and natural coverlet, attest to her skill. This piece was probably made on a loom in the basement of her two-story brick home (built in 1850 in the Ward's Cove area of Tazewell County), most likely from wool that came from her own sheep. Coverlet fabric was typically woven in one long piece the width of the loom (which in this case was about 29 inches), then cut into two or three sections that were sewn together to make the desired size. The maker often mismatched these, producing what some would consider an imperfect appearance that nonetheless reflected a personal style or preference. Such is the case with this bedcover, which Rebecca made in 1870; she gave it to her son, George Ward, who left it to his daughter, Mary Ward Bowen, who passed it to her daughter, Cecil Bowen Wendell.

Fig. 86. Woven overshot coverlet, wool and homespun linen, unknown pattern, 92½ x 74 inches, 4th quarter 19th century

This coverlet was made by Sarah Caroline Umberger Hedrick (who was known as Callie), another of the region's skilled weavers. The pattern of snowball clusters in horizontal bands radiates to a border, creating an overall appearance of wide stripes. Callie (who was from Wythe County, Virginia) was born just at the close of the Civil War, and married Joseph Washington Hedrick of Washington County, Virginia, in 1886. According to her family, she wove textile heirlooms using warp and weft threads spun from her own flax and local wool. This coverlet, ca. 1890, is one of seven she made for her husband's sister's children in Washington County, Virginia. Though it is more than a century old, it is still in mint condition (save for several slight stains), with strong linen and wool fibers and vivid rose, indigo, and green colors.

Fig. 87. Woven overshot coverlet, probably wool, cotton, and homespun linen, unknown pattern, 85 x 75 inches (approx.), 4th quarter 19th century
Margaret Susan Cecil Suttle, from Lee County, Virginia, made this rose and green coverlet, which has passed down through her family.

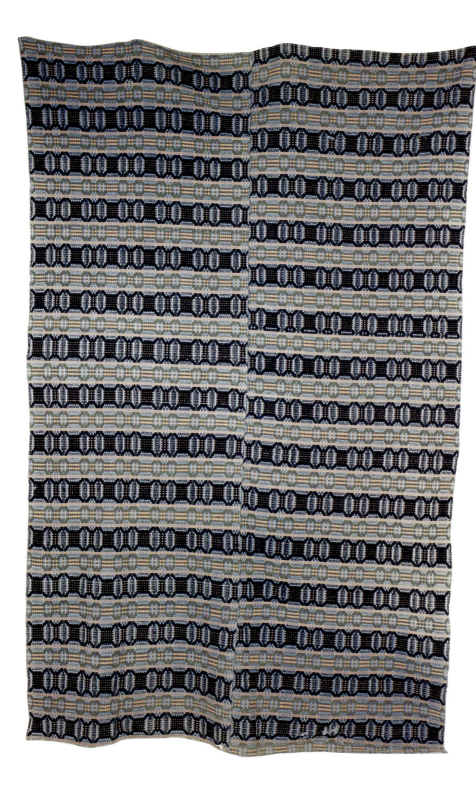

Fig. 88. Woven overshot coverlet, probably wool, cotton and homespun linen, 85 x 75 inches (approx.), 4th quarter 19th century
Indigo is the dominant color in this Lee County, Virginia, coverlet; the others are rose and green. It was made by Sarah Henderson Russell Evans and descended through her family.

Fig. 89. Woven overshot coverlet, probably wool, cotton, and homespun linen, 87 x 64½ inches, 4th quarter 19th century
This coverlet's tight pattern gives it an overall red appearance. It is made from two panels, each approximately 32 inches wide, and was found in Northeast Tennessee, its maker unknown.

Fig. 90. Woven overshot coverlet, probably wool, cotton, and homespun linen, 88 x 71½ inches, 4th quarter 19th century
This indigo and rose coverlet by an unknown maker is from Northeast Tennessee. Each panel measures 36 inches wide.

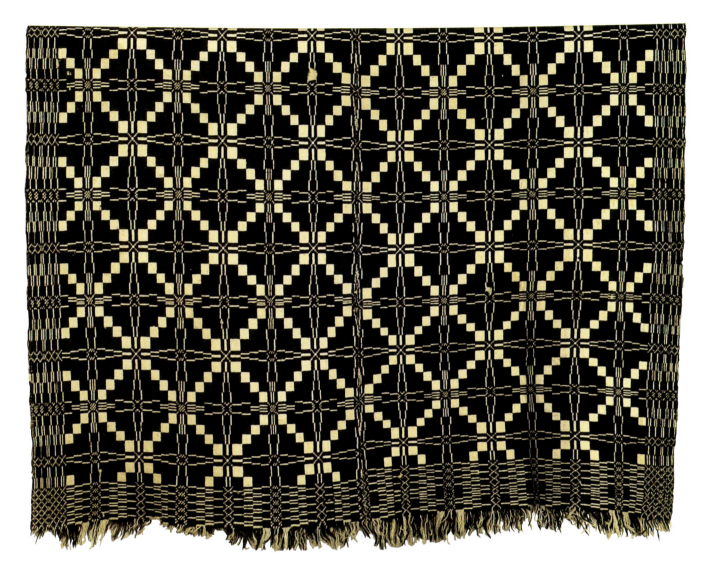

Fig. 91. Woven coverlet, double weave, wool and cotton, 90 x 69 inches, 4th quarter 19th century

Black-and-white coverlets are fairly uncommon in this region, as are double weaves. This example has descended through the David Gillock Rose family in Abingdon. It is made of two pieces of woven fabric, which essentially doubles the weaving and creates an extremely heavy bedcover that is also reversible. One side is predominantly black with white as the secondary color, while the other is white with black secondary.

Fig. 92. Pieced linsey-woolsey quilt, homespun linen and wool, 76½ x 63 inches, 3rd quarter 19th century

Margaret Ann Buckley Gobble (b. 1831) came from a family of home weavers in Washington County, Virginia. The Gobbles grew their own flax, which they spun into linen fibers to use as warp threads, while wool from their sheep was spun and dyed to make the weft. (Like many weavers, they may have occasionally purchased cotton thread to substitute for linen.) This linsey-woolsey, made for cold nights in the Virginia mountains, started with several whole pieces of home-woven wool and linen fabric that were cut into squares and pieced together to form a top. Another whole woven piece was used for the back, and the two were then quilted together with batting in-between. The Gobble women created a wide range of beautiful textiles—pieced cotton quilts, wool coverlets, crazy quilts, and clothing—many of which have stayed within the family for more than a century; this is one of at least two known examples of linsey-woolseys they produced. Margaret Ann's loom, which was located behind her home in the "loom house," also survives, at least in part: pieces of it have been made into a loom for her great-granddaughter, who carries on the family textile tradition.

Fig. 93. Linsey-woolsey quilt, homespun linen and wool, 80 x 70 inches (approx.), 4th quarter 19th century

This russet-colored quilt from Northeast Tennessee is an example of the whole-cloth linsey quilt, which is made from a whole piece of home-woven wool-and-linen fabric, backed by another with batting between. The three pieces are then quilted, in this instance with an overall fan design.

Fig. 94. Woven blanket, wool, 1st or 2nd quarter 19th century
This colorful blanket, with its pattern of intersecting stripes, is typical of a number documented in Southwest Virginia.

Fig. 95. Pieced quilt, cotton, version of "Christian's Cross" or "Grandmother's Pride" pattern, 84¼ x 97 inches, 2nd quarter 19th century
This is a rare example of a pre-1850 pieced quilt that has survived in mint condition. It was made near the Glade Spring area of Washington County, Virginia.

Fig. 96. Appliqué quilt, homespun and cotton, version of "Wreath of Roses" pattern, 90 x 80 inches (approx.), 3rd quarter 19th century
This quilt, which is in excellent condition, is still owned by the Lee County, Virginia, family of its maker, Sarah Henderson Russell Evans (who also produced the coverlet pictured in figure 88).

Fig. 97. Pieced quilt, cotton, "New York Beauty" pattern (local name "Bristol Beauty"), 108 x 108 inches, 3rd quarter 19th century
The Turkey reds and greens are still vibrant in this quilt, which was made by Susan Campbell Lowry in Washington County, Tennessee, near the Virginia border. These colors are also evident in another example of her work (see fig. 98).

Fig. 98. Pieced quilt, cotton, 87 x 78 inches, 3rd quarter 19th century
Susan Campbell Lowry stitched the date, 1883, into this quilt, which is typical of the intricate quilting stitches found in pieces she produced (see fig. 97).

Fig. 99. Detail of pieced quilt (fig. 98)

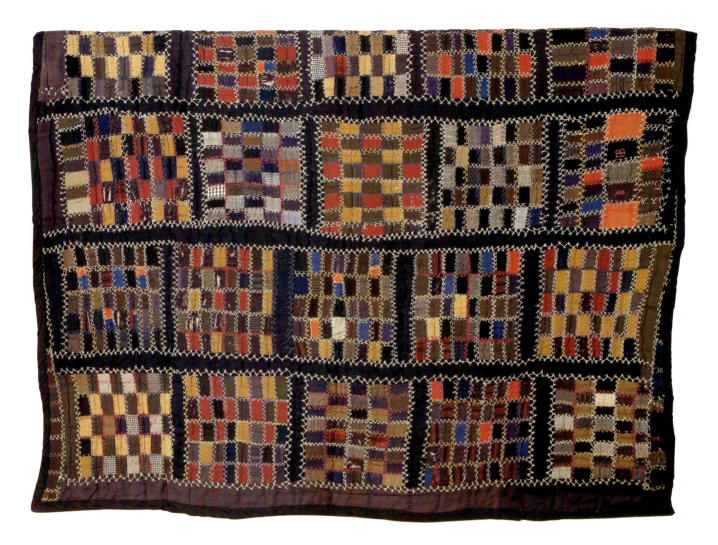

Fig. 100. Crazy quilt, wool and cotton flannels, 72¼ x 61 inches,
4th quarter 19th century
*Annie L. McGlothlin (1871–1937) made this colorful crazy quilt at her home
on Garden Creek in Buchanan County, Virginia, around 1890, when crazy
quilts made of cotton flannels were popular in America. This example is
made of multicolored squares pieced together into large squares to create
an "organized" crazy pattern. A running blanket stitch covers each seam.*

Fig. 101. Crazy quilt, silk and velvet with cotton backing, 69 x 69½ inches, 4th quarter 19th century

As was common practice, Katherine Sexton Sanders (from Smyth County, Virginia) embroidered her initials into this crazy quilt, which is made of silks and velvets. Usually referred to as "show quilts" (as they were meant to show off the quilter's skills), crazy quilts first became fashionable during the 1880s, and were often made to mark such important events as weddings. In many surviving examples, several sets of initials are worked into the fabric, either as a testament to those who contributed pieces to the finished product or as a record of relationships to the maker. This quilt is also embroidered with approximately thirty designs, most of which are floral, and features painted flowers and symbols as well. Katherine used silk thread and various small stitches to cover the seams. Unlike most crazy quilts, this example has been backed (with red cotton fabric); like all others, however, it is neither quilted nor has batting between the front and back.

Fig. 102. Detail of crazy quilt (fig. 101)

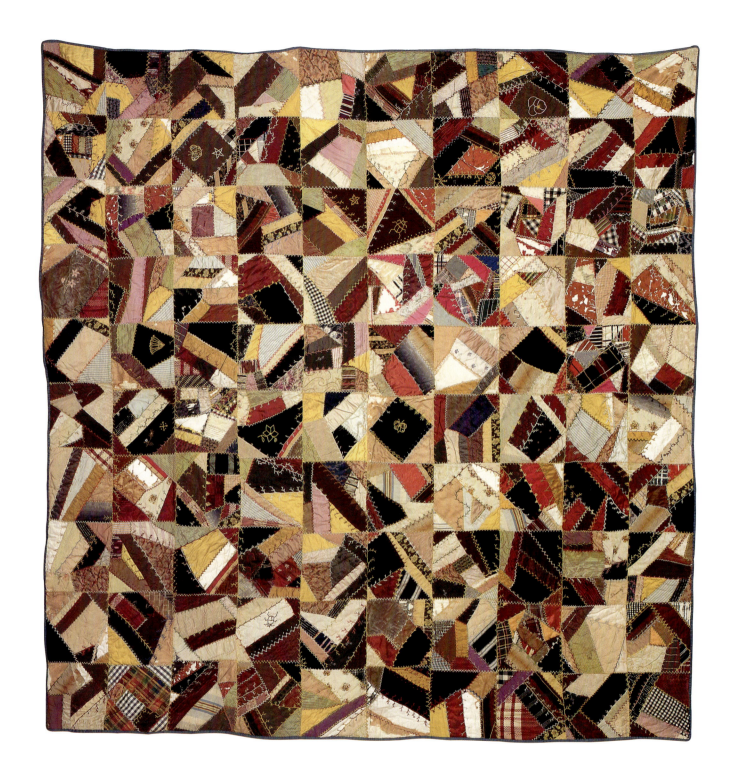

Fig. 103. Crazy quilt, silk and velvet, 77⅞ x 77½ inches, 4th quarter 19th century
This quilt was made by an unidentified member of the Litchfield and Penn families of Washington County, Virginia, who have kept it as an heirloom down through the years.

Fig. 104. Pieced quilt, cotton, "Double Wedding Ring" pattern, 86 x 63½ inches, 2nd quarter 20th century
An example of a twentieth-century pieced quilt, this is one of several made in Scott County, Virginia, by skilled quilter, Bonnie Hillman Bond (b. 1888). It is still in her family.

Fig. 105. Pieced quilt, silk, "Log Cabin" pattern, 64 x 52½ inches, 2nd quarter 20th century
This elegant quilt, with its hand-stitched top, is one of many made by Susan Essie Smith Houston from the Piney Flats area of Northeast Tennessee, a skilled seamstress who had an artist's eye for color and design. Made of squares comprised of precisely cut and chosen fabrics, its finished design includes diagonal stripes created by the repetitive placement of the pieces. Like many other quilters, Susan incorporated remnants of her daughters' dresses. After being cut to pattern, each square was sewn to a lightweight muslin-like fabric to produce the finished top. The maker's granddaughter, and present owner, tied the quilt to its silk back and created the border; there is no batting between the top and back.

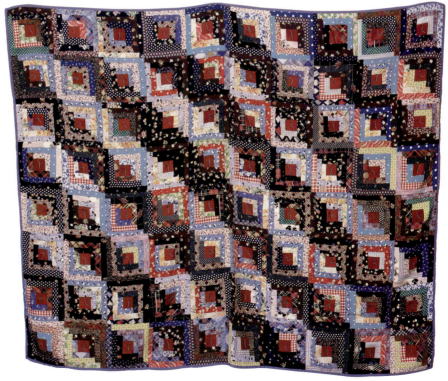

Fig. 106. Cross-stitched sampler, probably homespun and cotton, 23½ x 23½ inches, 2nd quarter 19th century
Samplers were produced to refine and to demonstrate the needlework skills learned by young girls. This example was stitched by a particularly adept thirteen-year-old, Susan E. V. Mountcastle, from Hawkins County, Tennessee.

Fig. 107. Dress, hand-dyed wool homespun, 3rd quarter 19th century
Millie Payne Jackson made this red plaid dress on the family farm in Richlands, Tazewell County, Virginia. The wool was shorn from local sheep, then spun, dyed, and woven to produce the fabric.

WEAVERS, SPINNERS, AND CARDERS

Sources: U.S. Population Census Records, 1850 and 1860; Industry Schedule 1860; and Washington Co., Va., newspaper abstracts (*Abingdon Virginian* 1872; *Democrat* 1855, 1858, 1859; *Political Prospect* 1812, 1815; *Virginia Statesman* 1836). Records include artisan information for the Virginia counties of Buchanan, Dickenson, Lee, Russell, Scott, Smyth, Tazewell, Washington, and Wise, and for the Tennessee counties of Carter, Greene, Hawkins, Johnson, Sullivan, and Washington. *Note:* More than sixty seamstresses are listed in Russell County's 1860 census.

Letter abbreviations following a date refer to the census (e.g., 1850C) or industry schedule (e.g., 1860I).

Addington, Harriet, b. Va., age 30, weaver, Scott Co., Va., 1860C

Aldridge, Sarah, b. Va., age 32, weaver, Scott Co., Va., 1860C

Alley, Mariah, b. Va., age 59, weaver, Scott Co., Va., 1860C

Anderson, Margaret, b. Tenn., age 69, weaver, Scott Co., Va., 1860C

Andrew, Sarah, b. Va., age 65, weaver, Scott Co., Va., 1860C

Bailey, Isabell, b. Va., age 39, weaver, Scott Co., Va., 1860C

Blevins, Clemma, b. Tenn., age 28, weaver, Sullivan Co., Tenn., 1860C

Bound, Margaret, b. Va., age 65, weaver, Scott Co., Va., 1860C

Briggs, Polly, b. [?], age 19, weaver, Washington Co., Va., 1860C

Buckley, Ann, b. Va., age 74, knitter and spinner, Russell Co., Va., 1860C

Burris, Patsy, b. Va., age 53, spinner, Russell Co., Va., 1860C

Calton, Rachel, b. Va., age 45, weaver, Scott Co., Va., 1860C

Carr, Katherine, b. Tenn., age 26, weaver, Carter Co., Tenn., 1850C

Carter, Amanda, b. Va., age 34, weaver, Scott Co., Va., 1860C

Carter, Elizabeth, b. Va., age 70, weaver, Scott Co., Va., 1860C

Carter, Elizabeth, b. Va., age 56, weaver, Scott Co., Va., 1860C

Carter, Mahalia, b. Va., age 21, weaver, Scott Co., Va., 1860C

Carter, Mary, b. Va., age 28, weaver, Scott Co., Va., 1860C

Carter, Susannah, b. Va., age 50, weaver, Scott Co., Va., 1860C

Casteel, Malinda, b. Va., age 48, weaver, Scott Co., Va., 1860C

Cawood, Mary, b. [?], age 18, weaver, Washington Co., Va., 1860C

Chafin, Lousanah, b. N.C., age 42, weaver and spinner, Russell Co., Va., 1860C

Clark, Sarah, b. [?], age 22, weaver, Washington Co., Va., 1860C

Cleek, Julia, b. Va., age 30, weaver, Scott Co., Va., 1860C

Collins, Joseph, b. Tenn., age 19, weaver, Sullivan Co., Tenn., 1860C

Collins, Nancy, b. Tenn., age 26, weaver, Sullivan Co., Tenn., 1860C

Collins, Priscilla, b. Tenn., age 34, weaver, Sullivan Co., Tenn., 1860C

Combs, Jane, b. [?], age 20, weaver, Washington Co., Va., 1860C

Combs, Sarah, b. [?], age 19, weaver, Washington Co., Va., 1860C

Cooker, Elizabeth, b. N.C., age 55, Scott Co., Va., 1860C

Cowder, Margaret, b. Va., age 43, Scott Co., Va., 1860C

Daniel, Becky, b. Va., age 61, weaver, Scott Co., Va., 1860C

Darnold, Ruth, b. N.C., age 48, spinner and weaver, Russell Co., Va., 1860C

Davenport, Eliza, b. Tenn., age 38, weaver, Washington Co., Va., 1850C

Davis, Margaret, b. Tenn., age 22, weaver, Sullivan Co., Tenn., 1860C

Davison, Mariah, b. Va., age 60, weaver, Scott Co., Va., 1860C

Dean, Elizabeth, b. Va., age 40, weaver, Scott Co., Va., 1860C

Dean, Nancy, b. Va., age 40, weaver, Scott Co., Va., 1860C

Dill, Amanda, b. Va., age 32, weaver, Scott Co., Va., 1860C

Dotson, Harriet, b. Va., age 15, spinner, Russell Co., Va, 1860C

Duncan, Jane, b. Va., age 39, weaver, Scott Co., Va., 1860C

Eakins, Lettis, b. Va., age 68, weaver, Scott Co., Va., 1860C

Edwards, Theneta, b. N.C., age 59, weaver, Scott Co., Va, 1860C

Egan, Elizabeth, b. Va., age 25, weaver, Scott Co., Va., 1860C

Everhart, Abraham, b. [?], age 37, carder, Tazewell Co., Va, 1850C

Faris, Ann, b [?], age 17, weaver, Washington Co., Va., 1860C

Felty, Catherine, b. [?], age 18, weaver, Washington Co., Va. 1860C

Flanery, Sarah, b. Va., age 37, weaver, Scott Co., Va., 1860C

Flanery, Sarah D., b. Va., age 22, weaver, Scott Co., Va., 1860C

Fleenor, Sarah, b. [?], age 23, weaver, Washington Co., Va., 1860C

Franklin, Margaret, b. Va., age 32, weaver, Scott Co., Va., 1860C

Frazier, Elizabeth, b. Va., age 16, weaver, Scott Co., Va., 1860C

Frazier, Nancy, b. Tenn., age 24, weaver, Scott Co., Va., 1860C

Frazier, Rebecca, b. Va., age 17, weaver, Scott Co., Va., 1860C

Frily, Nancy, b. Va., age 21, weaver, Scott Co., Va., 1860C

Fugate, Sarah, b. Tenn., age 43, weaver, Scott Co., Va., 1860C

Gillen, Mary, b. Va., age 56, weaver, Scott Co., Va., 1860C

Gillenwater, Nancy, b. Va., age 34, weaver, Scott Co., Va., 1860C

Gobble, Elizabeth, b. [?], age 18, weaver, Washington Co., Va., 1860C

Gobble, Mary, b. [?], age 23, weaver, Washington Co., Va., 1860C

Gobble, Suzanne, b. [?], age 19, weaver, Washington Co., Va., 1860C

Graham, Margaret, b. Va., age 35, weaver, Sullivan Co., Tenn., 1860C

Gray, Helvina, b. Va., age 46, weaver, Scott Co., Va., 1860C

Gray, Lucy, b. Va., age 20, weaver, Scott Co., Va., 1860C

Gray, Mary, b. Va. age 26, weaver, Scott Co., Va., 1860C

Grear, Elizabeth, b. Va., age 35, weaver, Scott Co., Va., 1860C

Green, Martha, b. Va., age 16, weaver, Scott Co., Va., 1860C

Hale, Jane, b. Va., age 30, weaver, Scott Co., Va., 1860C

Hale, Mary, b. Va., age 60, weaver, Scott Co., Va., 1860C

Hall, Patsy, b. Va. age 38, weaver, Tazewell Co., Va., 1860C

Hamilton, Margaret, b. Tenn., age 17, weaver, Sullivan Co., Tenn., 1860C

Hamilton, Mary, b. Tenn., age 20, weaver, Sullivan Co., Tenn., 1860C

Hammon, Mary, b. Va. age 24, weaver, Scott Co., Va., 1860C

Hamons, Melinda, b. Va., age 44, weaver, Scott Co., Va., 1860C

Helbert, Maria, b. Va., age 29, weaver, Sullivan
  Co., Tenn., 1860C
Helbert, Rebecca, b. Va., age 29, weaver, Sullivan
  Co., Tenn., 1860C
Herman, Margaret, b. [?], age 30, weaver,
  Washington Co., Va,. 1860C
Hickam, Elanor, b. Va., age 60, weaver, Scott Co.,
  Va., 1860C
Hicks, Elizabeth, b. Tenn., age 42, weaver,
  Sullivan Co., Tenn., 1860C
Hicks, Lizzie, b. Tenn., age 50, weaver, Sullivan
  Co., Tenn., 1860C
Hicks, Mary, b. [?], age 23, weaver, Washington
  Co., Va., 1860C
Hockett, Ellen, b. [?], age 38, weaver, Washington
  Co., Va., 1860C
Horn, Eliza, b. Va., age 18, weaver, Scott Co., Va.,
  1860C
Horn, Emily, b. Va., age 15, weaver, Scott Co., Va.,
  1860C
Humphreys, Catherine, b. [?], age 26, weaver,
  Washington Co., Va. 1860C
Hundon, Rachel, b. [?], age 20, weaver,
  Washington Co., Va. 1860C
Hutton, Martha, b. [?], age 18, weaver,
  Washington Co., Va., 1860C
Jackson, Nancy, b. N.C., age 53, weaver, Scott Co.,
  Va., 1860C
Johnson, Polly, b. Va., age 47, weaver, Scott Co.,
  Va., 1860C
Jones, Margaret, b. Tenn., age 19, weaver, Sullivan
  Co., Tenn., 1860C
Jones, Sarah, b. Tenn., age 21, weaver, Sullivan
  Co., Tenn., 1860C
Keith, Delila, b. Va., age 17, spinner, Russell Co.,
  Va., 1860C
Kenslor, Martha, b. Va., age 24, weaver, Scott Co.,
  Va., 1860C
Kernan, Polly, b. [?], age 23, weaver, Washington
  Co., Va., 1860C
Kernan, Sidney, b. [?], age 17, weaver, Washington
  Co., Va., 1860C
Kilgore, Vera, b. Va., age 28, weaver, Scott Co., Va.,
  1860C
King, Nancy, b. Va., age 20, weaver, Russell Co.,
  Va., 1860C

Lane, Hannah, b. Va., age 24, weaver, Scott Co.,
  Va., 1860C
Lane, Harriet, b. Tenn., age 17, weaver, Sullivan
  Co., Tenn., 1860C
Lane, Julia, b. Va., age 35, weaver, Scott Co., Va.,
  1860C
Lane, Margaret, b. Va., age 25, weaver, Scott Co.,
  Va., 1860C
Latture, Ester, b. Tenn., age 43, weaver, Sullivan
  Co., Tenn., 1860C
Latture, Mary, b. Tenn., age 16, weaver, Sullivan
  Co., Tenn., 1860C
Lawson, Nancy, b. Va., age 67, weaver, Scott Co.,
  Va., 1860C
Lingo, Susan J., b. Tenn., age 26, weaver, Sullivan
  Co., Tenn., 1860C
Logan, Sarah, b. [?], age 17, weaver, Washington
  Co., Va., 1860C
Maiden, Margaret, b. [?], age 19, weaver,
  Washington Co., Va., 1860C
Marn, Sarah, b. Va., age 62, weaver, Scott Co., Va.,
  1860C
Marrs, Robert, b. Va., age 30, carder, Tazewell Co.,
  Va., 1860C
Martin, [?], b. Va., age 45, weaver, Scott Co., Va.,
  1860C
Maxwell, Henry, b. Va., age 23, carder, Tazewell
  Co., Va., 1860C
McNeu, Martha, b. [?], age 20, weaver,
  Washington Co., Va., 1860C
Millard, Cordelia, b. Tenn., age 21, weaver,
  Sullivan Co., Tenn., 1860C
Millard, Timothy, b. Tenn., age 48, carder,
  Sullivan Co., Tenn., 1860C
Miller, Elizabeth, b. Tenn., age 36, weaver,
  Sullivan Co., Tenn., 1860C
Miller, Mary, b. Va., age 32, weaver, Scott Co., Va.,
  1860C
Miller, Mary, b. Va., age 17, weaver, Scott Co., Va.,
  1860C
Moore, Elizabeth, b. Tenn., age 31, weaver,
  Sullivan Co., Tenn., 1860C
Moore, Helen, b. [?], age 27, weaver, Washington
  Co., Va., 1860C
Morrison, Rachel, b. Tenn., age 36, weaver,
  Sullivan Co., Tenn., 1860C

Mullins, Nancy, b. Va., age 16, weaver, Sullivan Co., Tenn., 1860C

Neil, Elizabeth, b. Va., age 28, weaver, Scott Co., Va., 1860C

Pearson, Martha, b. Va., age 42, weaver, Scott Co., Va., 1860C

Penley, Temperance, b. Va., age 70, weaver, Scott Co., Va., 1860C

Pippin, Zachariah, b. Russell Co., Va., age 50, carder, Tazewell Co., Va. 1850C

Quillen, Ann, b. Va., age 39, weaver, Scott Co., Va., 1860C

Ramey, Mary, b. Va., age 48, weaver, Scott Co., Va., 1860C

Ramey, Nancy, b. Va., age 25, weaver, Scott Co., Va., 1860C

Repass, Thomas, b. Va., age 18, carder, Tazewell Co., Va., 1860C

Roberts, [?], age 24, weaver, Washington Co., Va., 1860C

Russel, Elizabeth, b. Va., age 20, weaver, Scott Co., Va., 1860C

Saddler, Mary, b. Va., age 60, weaver, Russell Co., Va., 1860C

Salling, Caroline, b. Va., age [?], weaver, Scott Co., Va., 1860C

Salling, Nancy, b. Va., age 18, weaver, Scott Co., Va., 1860C

Sapp, Martha A. E., b. Va., age 36, weaver, Scott Co., Va., 1860C

Shuff, Nancy, b. [?], age 30, weaver, Washington Co., Va., 1860C

Smith, Malinda, b. Tenn., age 46, weaver, Sullivan Co., Tenn., 1860C

Smith, Nancy, b. Tenn., age 52, weaver, Sullivan Co., Tenn., 1860C

Snead, Jane, b. Va., age 32, weaver, Russell Co., Va., 1860C

Stanley, Hanah, b. Va., age 23, weaver, Scott Co., Va., 1860C

Starnes, Sarah, b. Va., age 44, weaver, Scott Co., Va., 1860C

Steward, Ann, b. Va., age 69, weaver, Scott Co., Va., 1860C

Steward, Mary, b. Va., age 27, weaver, Scott Co., Va., 1860C

Taylor, Catherine, b. Va., age 35, weaver, Scott Co., Va., 1860C

Todd, Sarah, b. [?], age 20, weaver, Washington Co., Va., 1860C

Venable, Davis, b. [?], age 20, weaver, Washington Co., Va., 1860C

Vineyard, Canna, b. Va., age 28, weaver, Scott Co., Va., 1860C

Vineyard, Elizabeth, b. Va., age 23, weaver, Scott Co., Va., 1860C

Whitaker, Nancy, b. Tenn., age 21, weaver, Sullivan Co., Tenn., 1860C

Whorry, John, b. [?], age 32, carder, Tazewell Co., Va., 1850C

Wickam, Nancy, b. Va., age 69, weaver, Scott Co., Va., 1860C

William, Matilda, b. Va., age 32, weaver, Scott Co., Va., 1860C

Williams, Catherine, b. Va., age 47, weaver, Scott Co., Va., 1860C

Williams, Susan, b. Va., age 38, weaver, Scott Co., Va., 1860C

Worton, Nancy, b. Va., age 38, weaver, Scott Co., Va., 1860C

Wright, Polly, b. Va., age 47, spinner, Russell Co., Va, 1860C

4 ✍ Pottery

Fig. 108. Plate, earthenware
with lead glaze, 10¼-inch diameter,
3rd or 4th quarter 19th century
*Although tableware must have been made
locally, this plate is one of the few pieces
that have been found. It is attributed to
the Cain pottery, an early, long-running
pottery business established in Blountville,
Sullivan County, Tennessee, by Leonard
Cain (who was originally from North
Carolina). Either Abraham or Martin
Cain was likely the potter.*

Both earthenware and stoneware were produced in Southwest Virginia and Northeast Tennessee, with a concentration along the Great Road and its tributaries. Areas of high pottery production corresponded to several factors—proximity to river, clay, transportation, and market. Most local pottery was plain, with incised lines as its only decoration and its ovoid, bulbous forms tending towards simplicity, in keeping with its primary purpose of function rather than beauty. On occasion, however, a potter added decorative embellishments: earthenware received liquefied oxides of blacks, browns, and greens, while stoneware bore designs in cobalt blue. Many potters came from particular settler groups, intermarried with other potter families, and moved from one shop to another, which led to a characteristic look and style of pottery.

Vessels for every imaginable use were made, including jars, jugs, crocks, milk pans, churns, pitchers, honey pots, field jugs, and plates, and even such specialized items as inkwells, flowerpots, and cuspidors.

EARTHENWARE POTTERY

The earliest potters produced earthenware, which was usually lead glazed, its reddish-orange color readily apparent on the unglazed bottom of fired pieces. Two good local examples of undecorated earthenware are a plate and flowerpot (figs. 108, 109) attributed to the Cain pottery in Sullivan County, Tennessee. Decorated earthenware from the region is characterized by manganese-, iron-, and copper-oxide daubs, splotches, or dribbles applied under the glaze. In "Earthenware Potters Along the Great Road in Virginia and Tennessee" (which appeared in the September 1983 issue of *Antiques*), Roddy Moore named such decorated pieces "Great Road Pottery" (see figure 110 for an illustrative example). Sometimes the decoration was allowed to dribble, as a Washington County, Virginia, pitcher illustrates (fig. 112); this stylistic element is also seen in a jug from nearby Sullivan County, Tennessee (fig. 115). The Haun pottery in Greene County, Tennessee, is credited with making one of the most striking vessels (fig. 118) thus far found in the region. It features cross-hatched copper-oxide decoration, an unusual design for Northeast Tennessee and Southwest Virginia pottery.

Another unusual piece is a jar with lid (fig. 116), made in Smyth County, Virginia, near the North Carolina line. Here the potter used kaolin clay, rather than the usual local earthenware clay, giving the jar a light color. The piece was then polychrome decorated with oxide slip in a design not usually seen on local pottery, but related to Moravian pottery from North Carolina. The Moravian potters, who were known to get their lead from Wythe County mines, are thought to have influenced local pottery, and this piece seems to support that conclusion. Another vessel (fig. 121), with clear Smyth County provenance, is related in form, with its high pulled handles and general body size and shape. Yet another example (fig. 122), which was found in Tazewell County, Virginia, but carries family history in Smyth County, raises an interesting prospect of relationship.

STONEWARE POTTERY

After the middle of the nineteenth century, most potters switched to making stoneware, although some Tennessee potters continued to make earthenware, as illustrated by a Carter County vessel with a slip-trailed date of 1880 (fig. 123). The decision to abandon earthenware was clearly influenced by the known health risks associated with lead glaze and the merits of the more durable and less porous stoneware clay. Local stoneware fired to gray or brown and was usually given a salt glaze. Frequently, storage vessels and crocks had the capacity as well as the maker's name stamped on the body, and some vessels were embellished with cobalt decoration.

A crock or churn from Washington County, Virginia, (fig. 128) is a good example of local stoneware, both in form and color. Its lug handles are one of several treatments used locally, and its simple slightly bulbous shape is also typical. Like many stoneware vessels, it is stamped both with the maker's name, "Keys," and with "4" to designate its gallon size. The wide, thick rim suggests that it could have been a churn. Similar rims are seen on other crocks from Washington County (fig. 131) and from Smyth County, Virginia (fig. 132). These also illustrate local cobalt decoration applied as free-form flowers.

J. M. Barlow (who made the crock pictured in figure 131) was a typical example of the sort of potter who continuously moved around or worked in a number of places. He worked as a potter in the Osceola area of Washington County, Virginia, as well as in at least one other Washington County location, Alum Wells in the Mendota area. Examples of his pottery have been found with distinct stamps for each location. One example, a jar which reads "J. M. Barlow, Ocola VA" (fig. 130), relates to a similar piece stamped "J. B. Magee" (fig. 129). Analogous forms and cobalt decoration are evident in both Magee's and Barlow's work, and both jars are good examples of decorated stoneware from Washington County, Virginia.

Pennsylvania was a point of origin for many of the region's settlers, including some of its artisans. After working as potters in the northeast, Charles Decker, J. B. Magee, and James H. Davis all arrived in Southwest Virginia about 1870, possibly to go into business together. Charles Decker had worked in various places as a potter, including the Remmey Factory in Philadelphia; Magee was from New York and Maryland; and Davis came from Pennsylvania. All three appeared in the 1870 census of Washington County and seemed to be working together, with Davis living in the same house as Magee. They in turn were close by Decker, who had gone into partnership with the landowner, Augustus Mallicote, to start his pottery operation. Decker is an example of a local potter who moved his whole operation from one location to another. By 1873 he had left his associates and moved to

Washington County, Tennessee, establishing the long-running Keystone Pottery, where most of his work was produced. One stunning and large cobalt-decorated presentation piece, created in 1884 (fig. 139), attests to his skill.

Although Charles Decker's business thrived right into the twentieth century, most utilitarian pottery production had ended by about 1900. Some potters attempted to adjust to the changing market, which called for products tailored to the garden, the cemetery, and the whiskey trade, as illustrated by a flowerpot from Washington County, Tennessee, that was made circa 1890 (fig. 141). Most, however, simply closed their shops.

Fig. 109. Flowerpot, earthenware with lead glaze, 6 inches,
3rd or 4th quarter 19th century

*It is unclear whether this piece of earthenware was made by a member
of the Cain family or another artisan working at their pottery. Oral tradition
attributes it to one of two potters bearing the name Hinshaw (which
appears in census records as Hancher or Henshaw). Jessee Hinshaw
was born in North Carolina and undoubtedly learned his craft there—
some scholars think that Leonard Cain hired him to work at his pottery
around 1840. His son, William, was also an area potter. In addition to this
possible business connection, the Hinshaw and Cain families lived in close
proximity to each other and were related by marriage.*

Fig. 110. Honey pot with lid, earthenware with lead glaze, 12 x 6½ inches, 2nd quarter 19th century

This honey pot illustrates the regional use of liquefied oxides to decorate earthenware, applied as daubs, dribbles, or splotches. Here, manganese oxide has been daubed on the surface to create black splotches. The high iron content of the local clay, coupled with lead glazing, produced the characteristic orange color. This piece has a bulbous ovoid form with two pulled handles applied high and close to the body—traits that are typical of local pottery. A good example of what has become known as Great Road Pottery, it descended through a family in the Watauga area of Washington County, Virginia, carefully preserved with its original finial-topped lid.

Fig. 111. Honey pot, earthenware with lead glaze, 12 x 6½ inches, 2nd quarter 19th century

The striking similarities between this honey pot and the one pictured in figure 110 suggest that they were likely made by the same potter. The fact that this piece has also been passed down through a family in Washington County adds to the speculation. The flat mouth may have been designed to accommodate a matching lid. (Though it has topped the pot for many years, the current one is probably not original to it.)

Fig. 112. Pitcher, earthenware with lead glaze, 11 inches, 2nd quarter 19th century

This pitcher, another type of locally produced vessel, has the same bulbous form and manganese-oxide decoration seen in figures 110 and 111. On this piece (found in the Bristol area of Washington County, Virginia), the potter allowed the manganese splotches to dribble and added an extruded strap handle.

Fig. 113. Jug, earthenware with lead glaze, 15½ x 11 inches, 3rd quarter 19th century, incised "M A CAIN Jug Maid by A B CAIN 1869" at the base of the handle
This large jug has a triple thumbprint at the handle base and sine waves incised between two rings at the shoulder. Though a significant amount of glaze has been lost, it is an important piece because the inscription documents it as Cain pottery, referring to Abraham B. Cain, who made this jug for his nephew, Martin, at the family pottery in Sullivan County, Tennessee.

Fig. 114. Jug, earthenware with lead glaze, 4½ x 2½ inches
This small jug from Sullivan County, Tennessee, is attributed to the Cain potters. It features splotch decoration—here made with iron and copper oxides under a lead glaze—similar to examples from nearby Washington County, Virginia (see figs. 110–112). The two incised shoulder rings are common to Cain pieces.

Fig. 115. Jug, earthenware with lead glaze, 1st quarter 19th century, incised "John Wolfe 1826" beneath the handle
Though informed speculation attributes this jug to the Cain pottery in Sullivan County, Tennessee, it may have actually been made by a potter named John Wolfe, whose name appears below the handle. The accompanying date, together with doubts as to whether the Cain pottery was in operation as early as 1826, supports this possibility.

Fig. 116. Jar with lid, kaolin, 12 inches,
2nd quarter 19th century
*Found near the North Carolina border
in Smyth County, Virginia, this colorful
jar retains its original lid. It is made of
kaolin clay and features high pulled-loop
handles attached at the shoulder. The
unknown potter applied a polychrome
slip decoration of manganese and
copper oxides, which is characteristic
of Moravian pottery.*

Fig. 117. Jar with lid, earthenware
with copper-oxide overglaze, 8¼ inches,
2nd or 3rd quarter 19th century
*The lid, which is marked "9" and is
original to this Greene County, Tennessee,
jar, fits within rather than flush with the
rim—an unusual feature. The copper-oxide
overglaze gives the piece a greenish hue,
and either "23" or "28" is incised on the
shoulder.*

Fig. 118. Storage vessel, earthenware
with lead glaze, 12½ inches, 2nd or 3rd
quarter 19th century
*This vessel is both unusual and striking.
Stamped and coggled, it has cross-
hatched, copper-oxide decoration, and is
attributed to the Haun pottery in Greene
County, Tennessee. There were at least
two Hauns—Lewis M. and Christopher
A.—working there, both of whom were
born in Tennessee. C. A. Haun was
hanged in Knoxville in 1861 as one of the
Greene County "bridge burners"; the only
evidence that he was a potter comes from
a letter that he wrote to his wife from jail
one day before he died.*

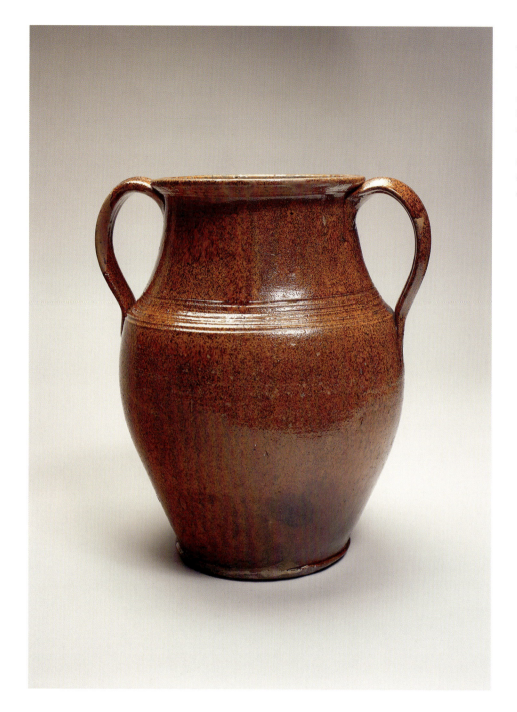

Fig. 119. Honey pot, earthenware
with lead glaze, 11 x 6½ inches,
2nd quarter 19th century
*This honey pot has two applied strap
handles, and its flat mouth suggests
that it may have once had a lid. Found
near the border between Smyth and
Washington counties in Virginia,
close to Glade Spring, it has a foot
and incised shoulder rings reminiscent
of those pictured in figures 121 and 122.*

Fig. 120. Inkwell, earthenware with lead glaze, 2½ x 3 inches, 2nd quarter 19th century
Local potters made a range of functional vessels, including inkwells. This example includes a central spout (complete with quill holder) that rises one inch above the body, which has four evenly spaced ⅛-inch holes interspersed by sets of three smaller openings. Lead glazing is coupled with daubed manganese-oxide decoration. The piece was passed down through a family on Smith Creek, off Route 700 in Washington County, Virginia.

Fig. 121. Storage vessel, earthenware with lead glaze, 12 inches, 2nd quarter 19th century
This ovoid storage vessel with large loop handles and thumbprint adhesion has clear provenance in Smyth County, Virginia. Its copper- and iron-oxide decoration is applied in a manner similar to that pictured in figure 122. (Though the lid appears to belong with this piece of pottery, it has long adorned and was documented with figure 111.)

Fig. 122. Storage vessel, earthenware with lead glaze, 12 inches, 2nd quarter 19th century
This vessel is an example of trailed manganese- and copper-oxide decoration, with indistinct markings that resemble the number 5 and letter X. It descended through a Tazewell County, Virginia, family with ancestry in adjacent Smyth County. Its large pulled handles are applied high on the shoulder, and the foot and general size and shape are similar to the pieces pictured in figures 116 and 121. The flat mouth indicates that it may have once had a lid.

Fig. 123. Crock, earthenware with lead glaze, 11½ inches,
4th quarter 19th century
*A late example of earthenware, this crock from Carter County, Tennessee,
boasts a floral design and the year "1880" in manganese slip decoration.*

Fig. 124. Storage jar, stoneware with salt glaze, 9 inches,
4th quarter 19th century, incised "Jessee Vestal 1880"

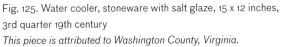

Fig. 125. Water cooler, stoneware with salt glaze, 15 x 12 inches,
3rd quarter 19th century
This piece is attributed to Washington County, Virginia.

Fig. 126. Water cooler, stoneware with salt glaze, 17 x 11 inches,
3rd quarter 19th century
*Unadorned (save for an X under the rim) and expertly fashioned with
clean lines and a graceful pouring mouth, this cooler resembles a large
pitcher. The only clue to its real function is the spout at the base. It was
passed down through a family in the Watauga area of Washington
County, Virginia.*

Fig. 127. Churn, stoneware with salt glaze, 18 inches, 2nd or 3rd quarter 19th century
This churn is embellished with incised straight and wavy lines around the diameter under the large lug handles (which have distinctive twists at the point of attachment). It was found in Wise County, Virginia.

Fig. 128. Churn or crock, stoneware with salt glaze, 14½ inches, 3rd quarter 19th century, stamped "Keys"

The thick rim suggests that this stoneware vessel might have been a churn. It is marked "Keys" just under the lug handle, with a visible "4" to the left and lines that have been incised under the rim. Records indicate that Robert Keys operated a pottery in the Glade Spring section of Washington County, Virginia, between 1860 and 1870. In 1860 he invested $200 in his pottery-making operation and employed two male helpers, who were paid $50 a month. His shop produced $1,600 in crocks and $400 in jugs that year. By 1870 he had three helpers and produced 3,600 gallons of stoneware, which sold for $600 (according to the manufacturer's schedule). He also ran a shop in the Osceola area. An 1871 adver-tisement in the Bristol News *referred to his pottery as the Osceola Stoneware Factory (Espenshade,* Potters on the Holston, *86; Moore, "Earthenware Potters," 536).*

Fig. 129. Storage jar, stoneware with salt glaze, 8 inches, 4th quarter 19th century, stamped "J. B. Magee"
This wide-mouthed vessel is one of many known Magee pieces. While most are unadorned, this is a good example of cobalt decoration, including the highlighted name stamp just under the rim. John B. Magee arrived in Washington County, Virginia, from the northeast at the same time as Charles Decker and James Davis (the three may have planned to go into business together). His shop was in the Osceola area, and his kiln site has been documented. He is listed as a potter in the 1870 population census, and by ten years later he and his son, Fred, were living next door to two other potters: J. M. Barlow and Alexander Harris (Espenshade, Potters on the Holston, *96; Moore, "Earthenware Potters," 536, 537).*

Fig. 130. Jar, stoneware with salt glaze, 12 inches, 4th quarter 19th century, stamped "J M Barlow, Ocola VA"

This wide-mouthed one-gallon crock features one of the two stamps used by J. M. Barlow of Washington County, Virginia. A bold incised line separates his name from the location, "Ocola." Though there is no evidence that Barlow owned any real estate in the Osceola area, he does appear in the 1880 population census, which lists him as a potter living near the middle fork of the Holston River, adjacent to Alexander Harris and John B. Magee. Magee likely employed him as one of four hands in his shop, and he also worked in another pottery in the Alum Wells area, where he marked his pieces "J. M. Barlow: Alum Wells." (Espenshade, *Potters on the Holston,* 89, 90).

Fig. 131. Crock, stoneware with salt glaze, 10½ inches, 4th quarter 19th century, stamped "JM Barlow"
The number "3," which indicates the gallon size, is stamped and highlighted in cobalt just under the potter's name on this piece.

Fig. 132. Crock, stoneware with salt glaze, 14 inches, 4th quarter 19th century
Stamped "3" to note its capacity in gallons, this crock features extensive cobalt decoration of free-form flowers. It has high lug handles, and its inner rim suggests it may have once had a lid. Though the maker is unknown, this stoneware vessel is attributed to either Smyth or Washington County, Virginia.

Fig. 133. Jar, stoneware with salt glaze, 7½ inches (4-inch diameter at mouth), 4th quarter 19th century
This small jar, cobalt decorated with a floral design, is from Washington County, Virginia.

Fig. 134. Pitcher, stoneware with salt glaze, 7 inches (4-inch diameter), 4th quarter 19th century
This small pitcher, which bears some resemblance to the jar pictured in figure 133, is also from Washington County, Virginia.

Fig. 135. Crock, stoneware with salt glaze, 9¾ inches, 4th quarter 19th century
The overall color of this Lee County, Virginia, crock is gray. Its unusual straight sides severely narrow before flaring, creating a rim that gives the piece the look of a milk can.

Fig. 136. Jar, stoneware with salt glaze, 8¼ inches, 4th quarter 19th century, stamped "E. W. Mort, Alums Wells, VA"

E. W. Mort was born in 1853 in the Strasburg area of Virginia's Shenandoah Valley, an area rich with potters. He practiced his craft during the last quarter of the nineteenth century, establishing his own shop in the Alum Wells area of Washington County, Virginia, prior to 1881. Sometime after 1893, he gave up the pottery business and became a Methodist minister. He died in 1923. Several complete pieces of Mort pottery survive, most of which exhibit the distinctive thin walls that "ping" when tapped. Mort's kiln site has been located; as an 1881 advertisement in the *Bristol News* notes: "Stoneware Alum Wells Pottery. I am now running to its full capacity the Alum Wells Pottery and am making and keeping on sale a full line of assorted stoneware, which will be sold at low prices. Merchant orders filled promptly and work guaranteed of fine quality. Flower pots and Vases furnished. I hope to receive a liberal patronage and would like them to test the quality of my Ware. Address, Ed. W. Mort, Alum Wells, Washington County, Va." (Espenshade, *Potters on the Holston,* 100; Moore, "Earthenware Potters," 528–37).

Fig. 137. Field jug, stoneware with salt glaze, 11 x 8 inches, 2nd quarter 19th century
This field jug from Washington County, Virginia, is cobalt decorated and has one handle and two spouts. The potter is unidentified, but the piece bears the mark "H."

Fig. 138. Poem jug, stoneware with salt glaze, 18 inches, 2nd quarter 19th century, incised "Jessee Vestal, 1849" (with an incised poem that reads "Long and Lazy, Little and Loud, Fair and Foolish, Dark and Proud, a Splendee Brandy Jug, Jessee Vestal, this is the 20th day of May, 1849")
This large jug, probably intended for display or presentation, was made by Jessee Vestal, who came from a family of potters near the Osceola area of Washington County, Virginia. The exact location of their pottery has never been determined.

According to the 1850 manufacturer's census, Thomas Vestal's pottery operation had a $200 capital investment, spent $30 on materials (firewood), and employed three hands (most likely Vestal himself together with John and James Wooten, members of another local potter family to whom he was related by marriage), producing an annual inventory of crocks valued at $1000. His son, Jessee, was born in Virginia in 1829 and died in 1904, according to his headstone in the Zion Methodist Church cemetery in Washington County (Espenshade, *Potters on the Holston,* 65–69).

Fig. 139. Exhibition crock, stoneware with salt glaze, 26 x 20½ inches, 4th quarter 19th century, stamped "Made by C. F. Decker, Proprietor of Keystone Pottery, Chucky Valley, Sep. 15, 1884"

Charles Decker was born in Germany and emigrated to America. He initially settled in Pennsylvania, where he worked at the Remmey Pottery Factory before establishing his own shop, which he called Keystone Pottery, in 1857. By 1870, he had moved to Southwest Virginia and was listed in the population census of Washington County, where he set up a pottery operation on land owned by Augustus Mallicote. He may have worked with two other potters, J. B. Magee and James H. Davis, who had arrived in the area from the northeast at about the same time. By 1873, he had relocated to Washington County, Tennessee, and there established a new business which he also named Keystone Pottery. This crock, made at the Tennessee pottery, features both stamped text and free-form design (Espenshade, *Potters on the Holston,* 80–84; Moore, "Earthenware Potters," 528–37).

Fig. 140. Cuspidor, stoneware with salt glaze, 3½ x 8 inches, 4th quarter 19th century, incised "Mrs. and Mr. J. H. Willis, Mar. 30, 1890, Greeneville, Tenn. Made at Keystone Pottery, Chucky Valley, Tenn." in script around the body

Fig. 141. Flowerpot, stoneware with salt
glaze and cobalt decoration, 4 x 7 inches
(approx.), 4th quarter 19th century
This piece is attributed to Charles Decker.

POTTERS

This list may seem small. Only those potters whose census information explicitly identified their occupation as such are included here; we also know that some potters were farmers and were listed by that livelihood. The size of this roster also reflects the fact that many potters included in the survey had not begun their local work by 1850–60, and early artisans had died or moved away.

Sources: U.S. Population Census Records, 1850 and 1860; Industry Schedule 1860; and Washington Co., Va., newspaper abstracts (*Abingdon Virginian* 1872; *Democrat* 1855, 1858, 1859; *Political Prospect* 1812, 1815; *Virginia Statesman* 1836). Records include artisan information for the Virginia counties of Buchanan, Dickenson, Lee, Russell, Scott, Smyth, Tazewell, Washington, and Wise, and for the Tennessee counties of Carter, Greene, Hawkins, Johnson, Sullivan, and Washington.

Letter abbreviations following a date refer to the census (e.g., 1850C) or industry schedule (e.g., 1860I).

Brown, John, b. Md., age 59, Tazewell Co., Va., 1860C

Cain, Abram, age 25, Sullivan Co., Tenn., 1850C; age 33, 1860C

Campbell, Joshua, age 34, Tazewell Co., Va., 1850C

Daugherty, Ezekiel T., b. Baltimore, Md., age 59, Russell Co., Va., 1850C

Hancher, Jessie, b. N.C., age 48, Sullivan Co., Tenn., 1850C; age 58, 1860C

Hancher, William, b. Tenn., age 21, Sullivan Co., Tenn., 1850C

Huston, William D., b. N.C., age 31, Sullivan Co., Tenn., 1860C

Keys, Robert, Washington Co., Va., 1860I

Myers, Thomas J., b. Va., age 43, Smyth Co., Va., 1850C; age 53, 1860C

O'Daniels[?], David, b. Pa., age 32, Carter Co., Tenn., 1850C

Russell, William, b. [?], age 37, Scott Co., Va., 1850C

Wooten, James, b. N.C., age 22, Washington Co., Va., 1850C; son of John Wooten

Wooten, John, b. N.C., age 47, Washington Co., Va., 1850C; according to Roddy Moore, b. 1803 in Iredell Co., N.C., father of James and John, with Wooten pottery shop

Wooten, Thomas, b. Tenn., age 32, Hawkins Co., Tenn., 1860C; listed as farmer, potter

5 ✍ Painting and Decoration

Not surprisingly, few artists were listed in nineteenth-century census records for the Great Road region. Particularly during the first years of the century, people had little time to think about painting anything beyond the color of their walls. Much of the decorative artwork created on the frontier was almost exclusively the legacy of itinerant artists, who braved the back roads and mountains of the newly settled territory to earn a living. Such artists traveled through the area, household to household, working primarily on portrait commissions supplemented by money earned applying decorative embellishments to interior architectural features, or creating illuminated family records and the occasional landscape painting.

By roughly 1825, the painting of portraits was in fashion on the frontier, and quite a few of these exist from this date forward. Portraits were considered a status symbol, and a number of early prominent citizens had their likenesses painted. Through midcentury, patrons sought out either

Detail of *The Powel Boys* (see fig. 150) by Samuel Shaver

the itinerant or the few local portrait painters, or chose to travel to established studios in eastern cities, often sitting for portraits when they were in town for business or political reasons.

TRAVELING ARTISTS

While most remained anonymous, some traveling artists signed their work. E. Ellis from Maine signed the portraits he painted of James Addison Peery, and his mother, Nancy Harman Peery, of Tazewell County, Virginia (figs. 142, 143), in 1845. Ellis, like others of his trade, took advantage of new opportunities for work in Virginia's backcountry in the period prior to the Civil War, when the region was experiencing vigorous growth in both population and economy. Amanda Patton Craig and her husband, James Chambers Craig, of Washington County, Virginia, also had their portraits painted (figs. 145, 146) during the early days of settlement. In this instance, as was more typical, the portraits remained unsigned, and we cannot be certain if they were painted locally. Another example of early portraiture is a painting of Rebecca Cecil Witten (fig. 147), from Tazewell County. Whether this was done at her home is not known, but it seems plausible given the difficulties of travel from her community.

LOCAL ARTISTS

By the end of the second quarter of the century, one census record lists a portrait painter in Abingdon and several other artists in the area. Samuel Shaver (ca. 1816–78) was one of the few locals who were successful artists. He focused his long career on painting portraits, primarily of Tennesseans. There is at least one Virginia portrait by him, of his uncle, Michael Shaver, a silversmith from Abingdon (fig. 148); this appropriately enough includes a silver-topped cane. Samuel Shaver's career as a portrait painter began in Sullivan County, Tennessee, probably as early as 1832, and spanned at least four decades. There are over one hundred known examples of his work. Gradually, the stark, plain style of his early portraits, evident in the painting of his uncle and in one of John A. McKinney (fig. 149), was replaced with a more refined style, and he began to add backgrounds, including animals, local scenery, and drapery. His portrait titled *The Powel Boys* (fig. 150) is an example of this later style.

Dora Alderson painted portraits much later, using nineteenth-century daguerreotypes to produce twentieth-century oil paintings (figs. 153, 154) of her long-deceased subjects. Many of these still exist, primarily from Russell and Tazewell counties, affording us a glimpse both of the ancestry of a number of local families and the successful career of this female Virginia artist.

DECORATIVE PAINTING

Decorative painting in the home was popular throughout the region beginning around 1825. Faux painting was applied on interior architectural features, including doors, moldings, mantels, and floors. The technique was known by a variety of names, such as grain or feather painting or marbleizing, and gave an inferior wood the rich-grained appearance of something finer. The artist used rags, feathers, corncobs, and combs to achieve the desired effect. Several original mantels (figs. 155–157), ca. 1830, survive as good examples of regional decorative painting from the Abingdon area and from Piney Flats, Tennessee.

Painted fireboards constitute a similar group of decorative artworks. Made to fit snugly within an empty summer firebox or to include the whole outside surround, they served as an attractive cover-up. Some were fashioned of horizontal or vertical boards on which the painted image was directly applied, while in others canvas was stretched on a wood frame and then painted, much like any work of art. A variety of devices kept fireboards in place, and they were often made to order, fit to a particular space. Although motifs included jars with greenery and flowers or stenciled images, many regional examples featured landscape scenes, as found on a Greene County fireboard (fig. 158). Many of the images were inspired by old paintings and prints, but occasionally a nearby locale or site was depicted.

Decorative records were a personal, intimate art form, usually meant just for the family. These private documents, like notes of important occasions kept in a family Bible, now and then received an artist's inspired touch, often that of a local minister, schoolmaster, or itinerant painter. Embellished with fanciful designs and colorful paints, most were works on paper, suitable for framing or tucking between the pages of a book for safekeeping. In all, the artist's brush was used to provide information about important details of life: birth, baptism, marriage, and death. Some area artists clearly developed a trade in commissions for illuminated family documents, as typical techniques and details, obviously from the same hand, are frequently seen. Four specific examples in Smyth County, Virginia, as well as a number of others in Wythe County (none pictured), suggest a fraktur tradition of calligraphy and decorative embellishment that reflects the German heritage of many settlers in this area. One artist in Tennessee created painted documents known as family records; a particularly colorful example (fig. 159) uses metallic paint, ink, and glitter to record the 1872 marriage of a Sullivan County couple, and the subsequent births (and one death) of their children.

LANDSCAPE PAINTINGS

A small number of landscape and still-life paintings from the area have been found, usually depicting local scenes. These date primarily from 1875, though several are from the first quarter of the twentieth century. Regardless of their relative scarcity, they are nevertheless an important local genre, as they provide the only surviving documentation of a number of noteworthy sites and places. Examples include paintings of the Smyth County Lincoln Wagon Factory (fig. 160) and of Witten's Mill in Tazewell County (fig. 161), and a Bristol street scene from 1880 (fig. 162) entitled "7th and State Streets."

 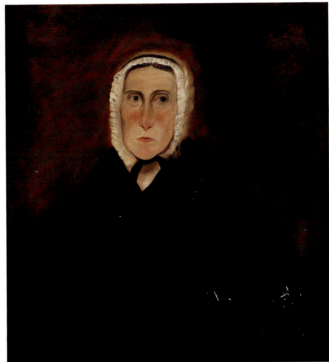

Figs. 142 and 143. James Addison Peery (1820–1902), and his mother, Nancy Harman Peery, oil on sailcloth, 26½ x 28¾ inches, 2nd quarter 19th century

E. Ellis, an itinerant artist from Maine, painted these portraits of two members of the Peery family, early settlers from Tazewell County in Southwest Virginia whose ranks included a Virginia governor.

Fig. 144. Robert Sanders (1792–1858), pastel on paper, 25½ x 20½ inches, 1st quarter 19th century

Robert Sanders was the son of William and Mary (Polly) Sanders, of Town House (part of a large tract of land that William and his brother, John, acquired through a business venture related to the saltworks in that part of Smyth County, Virginia). The Sanders family also had a stake in the lead mines in Wythe County, Virginia. Robert, who was called "Long Robin" because of his height, married Catherine Walker of Wythe County, with whom he had four children. The Town House ruin (see fig. 19), is still visible from Highway 11 in Chilhowie, Virginia. The artist who produced this portrait is unknown.

Figs. 145 and 146. James Chambers Craig (1793–1821), and his wife, Amanda Patton Craig (1796–1856), oil on canvas, 32 x 28 inches, 1st quarter 19th century

The Craig family was from Abingdon, and Amanda's father, Robert, was prominent in early Washington County affairs. These portraits were painted by an unknown artist, and it is uncertain whether their subjects sat for them locally.

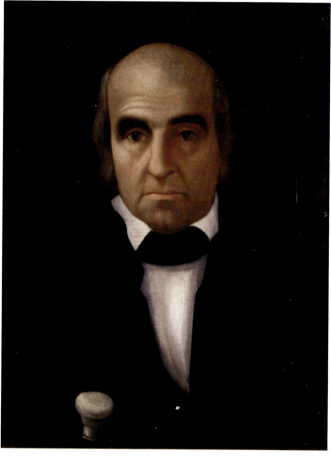

Fig. 147. Rebecca Cecil Witten (1765–?), oil on canvas, 30 x 28 inches, 1st quarter 19th century
A daughter of Samuel Cecil, from one of the first pioneer families of Tazewell County, Virginia, Rebecca Cecil was married to James "The Scout" Witten, a skilled woodsman and hunter. Her portrait was painted by an unknown artist.

Fig. 148. Michael Shaver (1775–1858), silversmith, jeweler, blacksmith, and dentist, oil on canvas, 24 x 18 inches, 2nd quarter 19th century
Samuel Shaver painted this portrait of his uncle, Michael Shaver, who was listed in Abingdon's census records as early as 1810. Surviving pieces of Michael Shaver's work provide the only documented examples of silver-smithing in the region (note the silver-topped cane). Samuel Shaver was a productive and successful portrait artist, leaving a legacy of more than one hundred portraits, primarily of Tennesseans.

Fig. 149. John A. McKinney (1781–1845), oil on canvas, 2nd quarter 19th century

This is one of Samuel Shaver's earliest known portraits, painted ca. 1842, probably in Rogersville, Hawkins County, Tennessee. John McKinney was born in Ireland and came to America in 1806, becoming a successful lawyer and landowner. One of his properties, the McKinney Tavern House, is today the Hale Springs Inn, one of Tennessee's oldest, continuously operated inns.

Fig. 150. *The Powel Boys,* oil on linen canvas, 67 x 67½ inches, 3rd quarter 19th century

This portrait by Samuel Shaver shows his later, more refined style and use of background images. Some of the University of Tennessee's buildings and the Tannery in Knoxville are readily identifiable. Typical of Shaver's paintings, the canvas is linen. The Powel boys—John (age 10), Kyle (8), Walter (7), and Thomas (?)—were the sons of John S. Powel.

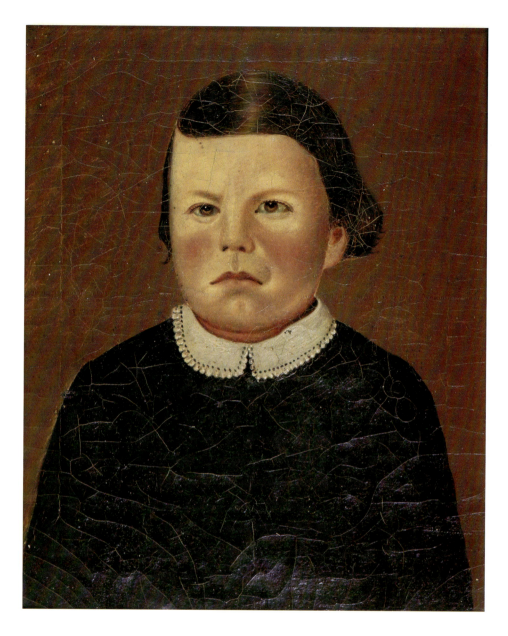

Fig. 151. William Grim (1790–1871), tinsmith, painted as a child, oil on canvas, 11½ x 9¼ inches, 4th quarter 18th century
The Grim tin shop operated on Main Street in Abingdon through much of the nineteenth century. William Grim was first listed in the 1830 census records of Washington County, Virginia. By 1850, he and his son David appear as tinsmiths in the Sullivan County, Tennessee, census. Ten years later, they are once again listed in Washington County, Virginia. These entries suggest that either the business had expanded across the state border to nearby Sullivan County or that the Grims had simply moved there for a while before returning to Washington County. The portrait, by an unknown artist, has descended through the family.

Fig. 152. Colonel Henry Bowen (1770–1850) and his granddaughter, Ellen Stuart Bowen (1835–59), oil on canvas, 2nd quarter 19th century
Colonel Henry Bowen was the son of Lieutenant Rees Bowen, who was killed at the Battle of Kings Mountain in 1780 (long considered a pivotal engagement of the Revolutionary War, fought and won primarily by the Overmountain Men of Southwest Virginia—then known as Washington County—and Tennessee). Colonel Bowen represented Tazewell County in the Virginia House of Delegates from 1802–6. The family attributes the tear in this painting to an incident during the Civil War, when five thousand hungry federal troops were encamped at the family home, Maiden Spring. The story goes that Ellen's younger sister, Louisa, who was annoyed with the soldiers, took two of their firearms up to the attic and dropped them down the space behind the walls. Equally irritated by this act of youthful defiance, a soldier slashed the portrait in retaliation. Louisa grew up to be an artist.

Fig. 153. Emily Thomas Patterson Hutcheson (1830–1914) and her daughter, Florine (1854–1930), oil on canvas, 40 x 25 inches, 1st quarter 20th century
Dora Alderson, a Russell County, Virginia, portrait artist, worked around the turn of the century and created a large body of work. Some of her commissions were for portraits of long-deceased ancestors, which she produced by using old daguerreotype images as her models. This is one example of this technique.

Fig. 154. John Taylor Smith (1805–62), oil on canvas, 26 x 21 inches, 1st quarter 20th century
This portrait of one of Russell County's early doctors was painted by Dora Alderson from a daguerreotype image. John Taylor Smith was educated at the University of Pennsylvania and practiced medicine on horseback throughout Southwest Virginia, where he was one of the first physicians to inoculate local patients for smallpox. His grandfather was Henry Smith, Long Hunter, surveyor, and member of the first court convened in Russell County, Virginia.

Fig. 155. Mantel, paint decorated, 56 x 73 x 7½ inches, 2nd quarter 19th century
From the Glade Spring area of Washington County, Virginia, this mantel is one of several original paint-decorated surfaces in the house, which was built around 1830. The mantel, with marbleizing covering the pine and popular woods, was probably painted by a traveling artist.

Fig. 156. Mantel, paint decorated, 55½ x 71 x 9 inches, 2nd quarter 19th century
This mantel was found in Piney Flats, Tennessee, and features gold feather painting over a rich brown base on black gum wood.

Fig. 157. Mantel, paint decorated, 2nd
quarter 19th century
*This heavily painted example of marbleizing
is still in its original location in Washington
County, Virginia.*

Fig. 158. Fireboard, oil on muslin within a large painted wooden frame, 42 x 44 inches, 4th quarter 19th century
Fireboards, like this one from Greene County, Tennessee, were either made to stand in front of the firebox or to fit within it. This example illustrates the common practice of making a surround for the painting, giving it the appearance of a framed picture.

Fig. 159. Cox family record, metallic paint, ink, and glitter on paper, 33¾ x 27¾ inches, 3rd quarter 19th century
In its original frame, this paint-decorated document records the marriage of James Cox and Jane Cordington on August 22, 1872 in Sullivan County, Tennessee, as well as subsequent births and the death of one of their children. William Carroll, Justice of the Peace, may have been the artist as well as the minister, as was sometimes the case. This particularly colorful family record, embellished with metallic paint, ink, and even glitter on a bright blue background, is one of two similarly decorated pieces that were found together. The text appears below a friendly "Home Sweet Home" and informs the reader: "This is to certify that James Cox and Nancy Jane Cordington were united in the Holy Bonds of Matrimony August 22 1872 at the Bride's Home in Sullivan County, Tennessee by William Carroll J.P."

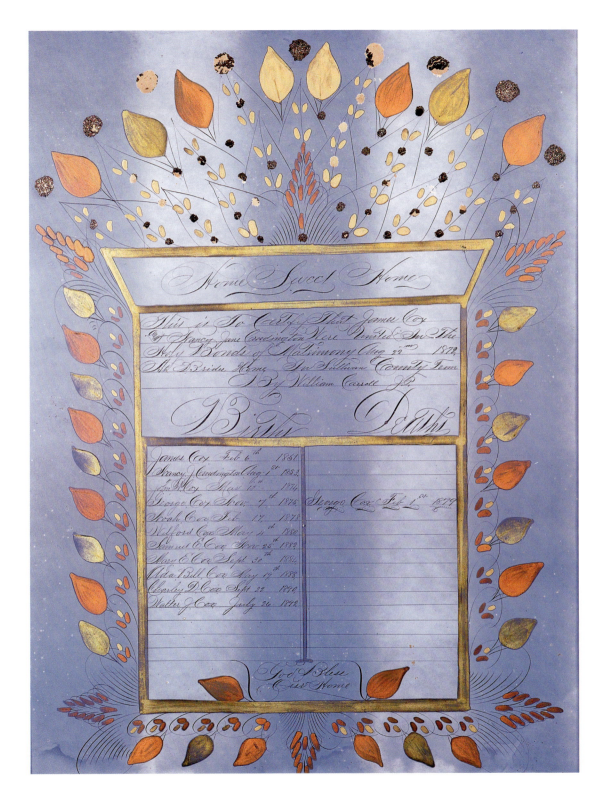

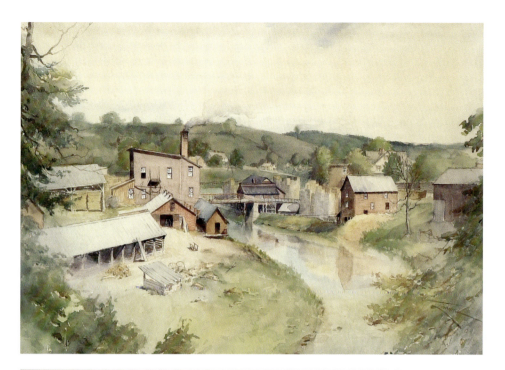

Fig. 160. Lincoln Wagon Factory in Smyth County, Virginia, watercolor on paper, 21½ x 30 inches, 4th quarter 19th century
This landscape is both a local example of an artist's work and a record of an early industrial site that no longer exists. The Lincoln Wagon Factory, which was located close to the Great Road in Smyth County, Virginia, near the town of Marion, was painted at the close of the nineteenth century by Charles Hardwick Lincoln (b. 1860), a relative of the factory owners who was visiting them from Massachusetts.

Fig. 161. Witten's Mill in Tazewell County, Virginia, watercolor on paper, 10 x 13 inches, 1st quarter 20th century
This scene, which was painted by an itinerant artist traveling through the area around 1920, features a mill and the surrounding locale in Tazewell County as they appeared at that time.

Fig. 162. Bristol, oil on canvas, 26 x 32½ inches, 4th quarter 19th century, marked "7th and State Streets"
This depiction of Bristol's main street was painted around 1880 by an unknown artist.

Fig. 163. Still life, oil on artist's board, 9½ x 15½ inches, 4th quarter 19th century
This still life includes a local newspaper, possibly the Abingdon Virginian, *and several letters. The facing envelope is addressed to Miss Grace Applegate, Martha Washington College, Abingdon, Virginia; the painting was done by Alice Baldwin, who was a student there. The college, which was established by the Holston Conference of the United Methodist Church and named in honor of Martha Washington, provided an education for young women from 1858 until 1932. It is currently the Martha Washington Inn.*

Fig. 164. Old Jonesborough Academy, oil on artist's board, 17½ x 23½ inches, 4th quarter 19th century
Josephine Darden painted this view of a school located in Jonesboro, Washington County, Tennessee.

Fig. 165. Natural Tunnel, Virginia, folding fire screen, oil on board, 1st or 2nd quarter 20th century
W. C. Coleman was a self-trained artist who worked in the Pattonsville area of Lee County, Virginia. During the early part of the twentieth century, he peddled his paintings of local scenes door-to-door. This three-section fire screen features one of Virginia's most important natural sites, the Natural Tunnel, which is located in adjacent Scott County. Coleman also produced paintings of other sites, using canvas made of old flour-sack material and his own handmade frames.

Although this list includes those individuals who were noted as "painters," there is no clear differentiation between a housepainter and one who worked on canvas. More research into other primary records may reveal which "painters," if any, were actually artists.

Sources: U.S. Population Census Records, 1850 and 1860; Industry Schedule 1860; and Washington Co., Va., newspaper abstracts (*Abingdon Virginian* 1872; *Democrat* 1855, 1858, 1859; *Political Prospect* 1812, 1815; *Virginia Statesman* 1836). Records include artisan information for the Virginia counties of Buchanan, Dickenson, Lee, Russell, Scott, Smyth, Tazewell, Washington, and Wise, and for the Tennessee counties of Carter, Greene, Hawkins, Johnson, Sullivan, and Washington.

Letter abbreviations following a date refer to the census (e.g., 1850C) or industry schedule (e.g., 1860I).

Bateman, William, b. Tenn., age 34, painter, Sullivan Co., Tenn, 1850C

Browalow, Henry, b. Va., age 22, artist, Washington Co., Va., 1870C

Brown, John M., b. Tenn., age 22, painter, Johnson Co., Tenn., 1850C

Brown, Joseph N. b. [?], age 30, painter, Lee Co., Va., 1850C

Carter, David A., b. Va., age 23, painter, Washington Co. (Abingdon), Va., 1850C

Clark, David L., b. Va., age 26, portrait painter, Washington Co. (Abingdon), Va., 1850C

Cooper, Jacob, b. Wythe Co., Va., age 36, painter, Russell Co., Va., 1850C

Dooley, Hiram, b. Va., age 45, painter, Washington Co. (Abingdon), Va., 1850C; also a chair maker, as revealed in newspaper ads in Washington Co., Tenn., *Nashville Whig* (1840) and in Washington Co., Va., *Democrat* (1858)

Henritze, Samuel, b. Va., age 25, painter, Washington Co., Va., 1850C

Hodges, Harry, b. Tenn., age 19, artist, Washington Co., Tenn., 1850C

Holt, Joseph, b. [?], age 30, painter, Smyth Co., Va., 1860C

Humphreys, Pleasant G., b. Tenn., age 23, painter, Carter Co., Tenn., 1850C

Hutcherson, William, b. Va., painter, Washington Co., Va., 1850C

Isaac, David, b. Washington Co., Va., age 19, painter, Russell Co., Va., 1850C

Johnston, Thomas, age 41, artist, Washington Co. (Abingdon), Va., 1860C

Johnson, Thomas, b. Va., age 37, portrait painter, Washington Co., Va., 1870C

Keen, J. W., b. Tenn., age 26, listed as daguerreo-typist, Sullivan Co., Tenn., 1850C

Kelly, B., b. Tenn., age 24, painter, Washington Co., Tenn., 1850C

Ketran, John, b. [?], age 21, artist, Washington Co. (Abingdon), Va., 1860C

Litteral, William J., b. Lee Co., Va., age 20, artist, Lee Co., Va., 1860C

Messick, Jacob, b. Va., age 54, painter, Washington Co., Va., 1850C

Messick, Jacob T., b. [?], age 45, painter, Sullivan Co., Tenn., 1850C

Messick, John, b. Tenn., age 21, painter, Sullivan Co., Tenn., 1850C

Moore, Richard, b. Va., age 27, "ambrotype artist," Sullivan Co., Tenn., 1860C

Morris, Robert, b. Ireland, age 70, painter, Carter Co., Tenn. 1850C

Painter, William, b. Va., age 38, painter, Hawkins Co., Tenn., 1860C

Paxton, Leslie, b. Tenn., age 29, painter, Carter Co., Tenn., 1850C

Powel, Samuel, b. Tenn., age 34, artist, Hawkins Co., Tenn., 1850C

Price, Joseph, b. England, age 37, [painter?], Sullivan Co., Tenn., 1850C

Radner, E. O., b. Tenn., age 43, painter, Sullivan Co., Tenn., 1860C

Ratcliff, Thomas B., b. England, age 53, painter, Tazewell Co., Va., 1850C

Russel, [?], b. Tenn., age 42, painter, Washington Co., Tenn., 1850C

Shaver, Samuel, age 34, artist, Hawkins Co., Tenn., 1850C

Smalls, Alexander, b. Tenn., age 22, painter, Hawkins Co., Tenn., 1850C

Tully, Cranford, b. [?], age 23, painter, Smyth Co., Va., 1850C

Wagner, Auston D., b. Va., age 15, painter apprentice, Johnson Co., Tenn., 1860C

Watkins, John E., b. Va., age 24, painter, Washington Co., Va., 1850C

Watkins, William G., b. Va., age 36, painter, Washington Co., Va., 1850C

Wolford, Jacob, b. Tenn., age 25, painter, Sullivan Co., Tenn., 1860C

[?], Andrew, age 26, artist, Washington Co., Va., 1860C

[? unclear name], age 21, artist, Washington Co. (Abingdon), Va., 1860C

6 ～✒ Metalwork

Wrought and Cast Iron, Tin, Silver, Guns

Metalsmiths accounted for a large number of artisans in the early days of settlement. Although silversmiths are listed in the 1850 and 1860 census records of Washington and Smyth counties in Virginia, as well as Washington, Hawkins, and Sullivan counties in Tennessee, only the work of Michael Shaver, who plied his trade in Abingdon between 1810 and 1858, has been documented (figs. 166–168). Other kinds of smiths, who made everything from hinges to wheels to nails, fill the lines for occupations in both census records. Wrought and cast iron products were made for everyday household use, including very early items like fat lamps (figs. 172, 173). Tin and coppersmiths were hardly numerous but were found in several counties, with a concentration in Abingdon. The Grim tin shop was a father-and-son operation there through much of the nineteenth century, even expanding at one point into Tennessee. Tin products locally produced included lamps, candle molds,

Fig. 166. Spoon, coin silver, 5½ inches, 1st or 2nd quarter 19th century, marked "MShaver" on reverse of handle *Michael Shaver was a silversmith in Abingdon. This spoon has continuous provenance in Abingdon, making it a good reference. (A portrait of Shaver, painted by his nephew, Samuel, appears in figure 148.)*

Fig. 167. Reverse of coin-silver spoon (fig. 166), showing Shaver mark

muffineers (fig. 177), and possibly even punch-decorated panels for safes. Gunsmiths, necessary artisans on Virginia and Tennessee's early frontier, made the local version of the half-stock rifle (figs. 178–180).

Fig. 168. Silver grouping: four wine goblets, baby's mug, teaspoon, sugar shovel, and child's feeder, 1st or 2nd quarter 19th century
This group is marked and attributed to Michael Shaver.

Figs. 169 and 170. Andirons, wrought iron,
14 inches, 1st or 2nd quarter 19th century
*These two sets of andirons are examples
of local ironwork produced for everyday
use. Their light form and stylized motifs
feature ram's heads and inverted hearts,
which lend them an artistic touch and
relate them to each other. Both were
made early on, during the first half of
the nineteenth century.*

Fig. 171. Fireplace tools, wrought iron, all 36 inches (approx.), 1st quarter 19th century

This shovel, log hook, and peel (from left to right) are examples of ordinary household objects made in the region.

Fig. 172. Cruise lamp, wrought iron,
5 inches (approx.), 4th quarter 18th
or 1st quarter 19th century
*A very early form of lighting for the
frontier, this Lee County, Virginia, fat
lamp burned a wick floating in grease.*

Fig. 173. Cruise lamp, wrought iron,
7 inches (approx.), 1st quarter 19th century
*This is a double-wick fat lamp (as is
evident by the two spouts) from
Washington County, Virginia.*

Fig. 174. Plate, cast iron, 9-inch diameter, 1st quarter 19th century
Though many must have been made, this iron plate is one of the few known. It is from either Smyth or Washington County, Virginia.

Fig. 175. Trivet, cast iron, 11 inches (5½-inch diameter), 1st quarter 19th century
The swirling fylfot design of this trivet, from Washington County, Tennessee, also appears on pierced-tin panels (see fig. 38).

Fig. 176. Candle lantern, tin, 14 inches
(5½-inch diameter), 1st or 2nd quarter
19th century
*A tinner from Johnson County, Tennessee,
produced this lantern, with a technique
identical to that used for pierced-tin safe
panels.*

Fig. 177. Tin grouping: 36-space candle mold with handle, 10¼ x 14 inches (right); muffineer or flour shaker, 3¾ x 2½ inches with ⅛-inch holes in lid (left); footed cheese press, 2½ inches (5-inch diameter) with ⅛-inch holes sides and bottom (center); 3rd quarter 19th century

Abingdon had several tinshops during the middle of the century. This group of housewares was made at the Grim tinshop; its provenance is clear, as the pieces descended through the tinsmith's family. (A portrait of William Grim appears in figure 151.)

Fig. 178. Half-stock rifle, curly maple and brass, 57¼ inches, 3rd quarter 19th century

John M. Whitesides was born in present-day Rockbridge County, the son of a clockmaker and grandson of a gun- and silversmith. He moved to Washington County, Virginia, during the second quarter of the nineteenth century and established a gunshop, where this .36 caliber rifle, with back-action ignition, percussion, and an oval inlay, was probably produced.

Fig. 179. Half-stock rifle, curly maple and silver, 56½ inches, 3rd quarter 19th century

This back-action-ignition, percussion, .36-caliber rifle, with German silver mountings and diamond-shaped inlay, was made by James Curtis Parker, a Scott County, Virginia, gunsmith.

Fig. 180. Half-stock rifle, curly maple, brass, and pewter, 52 inches, 3rd quarter 19th century, signed "O. A. G."

O. A. Grubb, a gunsmith from Washington County, Virginia, made this front-action-ignition, percussion, .38-caliber half-stock rifle, which has brass mountings and a pewter nose cap.

METALSMITHS

Blacksmiths and ironmongers were numerous in every county's census records. They have not been included in this list as we have not considered most of their products (nails, hinges, horseshoes, etc.) in our survey.

Sources: U.S. Population Census Records, 1850 and 1860; Industry Schedule 1860; and Washington Co., Va., newspaper abstracts (*Abingdon Virginian* 1872; *Democrat* 1855, 1858, 1859; *Political Prospect* 1812, 1815; *Virginia Statesman* 1836). Records include artisan information for the Virginia counties of Buchanan, Dickenson, Lee, Russell, Scott, Smyth, Tazewell, Washington, and Wise, and for the Tennessee counties of Carter, Greene, Hawkins, Johnson, Sullivan, and Washington.

Letter abbreviations following a date refer to the census (e.g., 1850C) or industry schedule (e.g., 1860I).

Atkinson, W., b. N.C., age 57, silversmith, Washington Co., Tenn., 1850C

Bailie, James P., b. Va., age 16, tinner, Washington Co. (Abingdon), Va., 1850C

Barr, Edwin, b. [?], age 27, tinner, Tazewell Co., Va., 1850C

Baugh, Caleb, b. Va., age 42, silversmith, Washington Co. (Abingdon), Va., 1850C; age 51, 1860C

Baugh, Valentine, b. Va., age 75, silversmith, Washington Co. (Abingdon), Va., 1850C

Bennett, Robert, b. Tenn., age 32, silversmith, Scott Co., Va., 1860C

Bowers, George, b. Mass., age 18, tinner, Washington Co. (Abingdon), Va., 1850C

Brownlow, Thomas G, b. Va., age 23, tinner, Hawkins Co., Tenn., 1860C

Burn, Joseph, b. Pa., 34, silversmith, Sullivan Co., Tenn., 1860C

Campbell, Alexander, b. Va., age 50, silversmith, Smyth Co., Va., 1860C

Fullen, James, b. Va., age 58, tin and coppersmith, Washington Co., Va., 1850C; age 69, listed as tin and coppersmith, Russell Co., Va., 1860C

Gates, Thomas, b. Va., age 31, tinner, Carter Co., Tenn., 1850C

Giles, John, b. Va., age 22, tinner, Washington Co. (Abingdon), Va., 1850C

Grim, David, b. Va., age 21, coppersmith, Sullivan Co., Tenn., 1850C; age 30, tin and coppersmith, Washington Co. (Abingdon), Va., 1860C

Grim, David, b. Va., age 21, tinner, Washington Co. (Abingdon), Va., 1850C

Grim, William, b. Va., age 56, tinner, Sullivan Co., Tenn., 1850C; age 69, tin and coppersmith, Washington Co. (Abingdon), Va, 1860C; listed in Washington Co., Va., 1830C

Hickey, Timothy M., b. Tenn., age 24, tinsmith, Johnson Co., Tenn., 1850C

Hirity, William, b. [?], age 29, tinner, Smyth Co., Va. 1850C

Killen, William N., b. [?], age 27, tinsmith, Washington Co. (Abingdon), Va., 1860C

Johnston, James, b. [?], age 21, tin and coppersmith, Washington Co. (Abingdon), Va., 1860C

Jones, A. S., b. Miss. [?], age 27, silversmith, Sullivan Co., Tenn., 1860C

Maxwell, Samuel, b. Ireland, age 65, coppersmith, Washington Co., Tenn., 1850C

McFalridge, Alf, b. Va., age 29, tinner, Tazewell Co., VA, 1850C

Miles, John H., b. Va., age 36, coppersmith, Washington Co. (Abingdon), Va., 1850C

Miller, John, b. Tenn., age 39, silversmith, Hawkins Co., Tenn., 1850C

Myler, John H., b. Va., age 36, coppersmith, Washington Co. (Abingdon), Va., 1850C

[?]Rye, John, b. [?], age 63, silversmith, Washington Co., Va., 1860C

Sears, David, Mass., age 36, tin and coppersmith, Washington Co. (Abingdon), Va. 1850C

Shaver, Michael, b. N.C., age 75, dentist (documented silversmith), Washington Co. (Abingdon), Va., 1850C

Wax, Henry G., b. Tenn., age 42, tinner, Hawkins Co., Tenn., 1860C

Wax, Jacob, b. Va., age 63, coppersmith, Hawkins Co., Tenn., 1850C

Wright, [?] A., b. Va., age 62, silversmith, Smyth Co., Va., 1860C

GUNSMITHS

Barkhimer, James, b. [?], age 21, Tazewell Co., Va., 1850C

Barkhimer, John, b. [?], age 22, Tazewell Co., Va., 1850C

Barkhimer, Thomas, b. [?], age 45, Tazewell Co., Va., 1850C

Beals, William H., b. Tenn., age 28, Washington Co., Tenn., 1850C

Clauson, Robert E., b. Washington Co., Va., age 51, Lee Co., Va., 1860C

Cole, James, b. Tenn., age 24, Sullivan Co., Tenn., 1860C

Copps, Jordan, b. N.C., age 45, gun stocker, Hawkins Co., Tenn., 1850C

Dangerfield, Leonard, b. Va., age 44, Tazewell Co., Va., 1850C; age 58, 1860C

Douglas, Jacob, b. Tenn., age 52, Washington Co., Tenn., 1850C; age 62, Sullivan Co., Tenn. 1860C

Douglas, John B., b. Tenn., age 26, Sullivan Co., Tenn., 1860C

Dugger, James B., b. Tenn., age 29, Johnson Co., Tenn., 1850C

Duncan, Alfred, b. Tenn., age 46, Sullivan Co., Tenn., 1850C

Dyer, Benjamin, b. N.C., age 39, Carter Co., Tenn., 1850C

Engle, Christian, b. [?], age 33, Tazewell Co., Va., 1850C

Engle, Ezra, b. Md., age 59, Tazewell Co., Va., 1850C

Forrester, John, b. [?], age 48, Tazewell Co., Va., 1850C

Forrester, John, b. [?], age 22, Tazewell Co., Va., 1850C

Fowler, Sampson, b. Tenn., age 55, Washington Co., Tenn., 1850C

Glover, Samuel, b. Tenn., age 31, Sullivan Co., Tenn., 1860C

Gobble, John, b. [?], age 45, Washington Co. (Abingdon), Va., 1860C

Gobble, Sam, b. [?], age 42, Washington Co. (Abingdon), Va., 1860C

Gross, Jacob, b. Tenn., age 70, Sullivan Co., Tenn., 1860C

Honaker, James/Isaac, b. Russell Co., Va., age 40, Russell Co., Va., 1850C

Lewis, Isaac, b. N.C., age 31, Carter Co., Tenn., 1850C

Lewis, Lawson, b. Tenn., age 20, Carter Co., Tenn., 1850C

Lewis, William S., b. Tenn., age 18, apprentice, Carter Co., Tenn., 1850C

Oxford, Samuel, b. N.C., age 59, Lee Co., Va., 1850C

Parks, William, b. Tenn., age 45, Washington Co., Tenn., 1850C

Rakes, Levi, b. Va., age 41, Tazewell Co., Va., 1850C

Sanders, Fred, Sr., b. S.C., age 61, Scott Co., Va., 1850C; age 70, 1860C (as Saunders)

Whitesides, John M., b. Rockbridge Co., Va., Washington Co., Va., 1850C (written "Whitndy"); age 51, 1860C

Whitlock, George H., b. Tenn., age 36, Washington Co., Tenn., 1850C

Whitlock, John, b. Tenn., age 25, Washington Co., Tenn., 1850C

Young, John, b. [?], age 38, Smyth Co., Va., 1850C

7 ∞ Baskets

Baskets of various types have been made throughout the region from the time of earliest settlement well into the twentieth century. Their forms have changed little through the years. The materials used to weave them—split oak, rye, honeysuckle, and straw—were all found locally. Most basket makers have remained unnamed, as they rarely signed their work. They made most of their products for family members or friends, including picnic baskets and storage baskets for eggs or feathers. Preferred local shapes included round and rectangular; sizes ranged from tiny to very large, as with a round coiled rye basket from Washington County, Virginia (fig. 181), that has survived in almost mint condition from the first half of the nineteenth century. An unusual football-shaped basket form is illustrated by an example from Dickenson County, Virginia (fig. 182), probably made for sowing grain or seeds.

For the most part, the same forms were made throughout the region with little variation. For example, the buttocks basket, which is found in abundance, has been documented in many sizes, from a small four-inch-wide example (fig. 185) to a very large one documented in Dickenson County, Virginia, that measures approximately 24 inches at its widest point. Tall baskets with lids (fig. 183) were made to store feathers for stuffing bed ticks (as many pounds were needed to properly fill a bed). These baskets, which were often painted, could have also been used for laundry.

Twentieth-century basket forms are similar to their older counterparts. "Colonel" Payne of Lee County, Virginia, exemplifies the enduring traditions of basket makers. This modern rural artisan peddled his distinctive woven round and rectangular baskets through the middle of the century, remarking to his buyers that he was keeping up a family tradition (fig. 188). His baskets feature a walnut-dyed weave set in the split-oak bands.

Fig. 182. Sowing basket, split oak, 14 x 9 inches, 1st quarter 20th century
It is generally believed that this acorn or football-shaped basket, from the Clintwood area of Dickenson County, Virginia, was made for sowing grain.

BASKETMAKERS

Sources: U.S. Population Census Records, 1850 and 1860; Industry Schedule 1860; and Washington Co., Va., newspaper abstracts (*Abingdon Virginian* 1872; *Democrat* 1855, 1858, 1859; *Political Prospect* 1812, 1815; *Virginia Statesman* 1836). Records include artisan information for the Virginia counties of Buchanan, Dickenson, Lee, Russell, Scott, Smyth, Tazewell, Washington, and Wise, and for the Tennessee counties of Carter, Greene, Hawkins, Johnson, Sullivan, and Washington.

Letter abbreviations following a date refer to the census (e.g., 1850C) or industry schedule (e.g., 1860I).

Bowlin, Amos, b. Russell Co., Va., age 36, Russell Co., Va., 1850C
Lasley, William, b. [?], age 75, Russell Co., Va., 1850C
Oxendine, Charles, b. Tenn., age 36, Hawkins Co., Tenn., 1850C

Fig. 183. Feather basket with lid, split oak, 30 x 16 inches, 4th quarter 19th century
Most likely intended to hold feathers for stuffing bed ticks, this basket still has its lid and handles, as well as its old paint (which was once probably white and has faded to gray). It was found in Washington County, Virginia.

Fig. 184. Egg-gathering basket, split oak, 5¾ x 13½ inches, 1st quarter 20th century
Round baskets are common throughout the region. This one, from Greene County, Tennessee, has distinguishing wrapped and notched double-rim bands and a convex bottom.

Fig. 185. Small buttocks basket, 4 inches, 1st quarter 20th century
This basket illustrates a form made consistently in all parts of Southwest Virginia and Northeast Tennessee. Examples of varying sizes have been found, from this diminutive piece to a larger version from Dickenson County, Virginia, which measures 24 inches across the top.

Fig. 186. Picnic basket with lid, 13 x 16 x 10 inches, 2nd quarter
20th century, signed "Will Tripplett, Dec. 1934 Benhams, Va."
This Washington County, Virginia, basket has a double hinged top.

Fig. 187. Round basket, split oak, 12 x 12 inches (7½ inches at rim), 4th quarter 19th century
This round basket with handle, similar to the one pictured in figure 184, descended through a family of early settlers in the Watauga area of Washington County, Virginia.

Fig. 188. Round basket, split oak, 10 inches (approx.), 2nd quarter 20th century
This example of a twentieth-century basket illustrates a classic standard round form with the addition of a walnut-dyed weave at the bottom third. This distinctive feature has been attributed to "Colonel" Payne of the Robins Chapel area of Lee County, Virginia.

8 ❧ Musical Instruments

Banjos, dulcimers, fiddles, and guitars have all played a part in the musical and decorative arts history of Southwest Virginia and Northeast Tennessee, and helped to create a cultural heritage that has become widely known through its contemporary traditions of bluegrass and country music. Banjos (which arrived with African slaves) and dulcimers (brought from Germany and Switzerland) were both adapted and made locally. Fiddles and guitars were also produced and played, although none made locally before 1925 were documented during the survey.

The dulcimer's recognizable long narrow form was interpreted slightly different by each maker, some teardrop shaped and others more rounded or squared. Banjos, too, varied according to the maker, though all used hides stretched over wooden frames with metal and wooden pegs and frets. Most instrument makers catered to family and friends, and thus stories and family histories are sometimes the only way to document these artisans.

Fig. 189. Banjo, made by Bill Plummer (left); dulcimer, made by Testerman (center); banjo, made by Nora Goode (right)

Fig. 190. Banjo, wood and hide head,
4th quarter 19th century
Bill Plummer, the maker of this banjo,
was a multitalented African American
from Smyth County, Virginia, who was
also a mechanic, inventor, and cabinet-
maker (see also figs. 59, 189). He
decorated this fine example with red
paint and white stars.

Fig. 191. Banjo, wood and hide head, 36 inches (12¾-inch head), 1st quarter 20th century, marked "SMS"

This banjo, which features a 36-bracket head and 6 strings, was made by Silas Mitchell Suttle of Lee County, Virginia. The fret board is one piece of copper crimped to mark the divisions.

Fig. 192. Banjo, wood and hide head,
4th quarter 19th century
*Nora Goode of Smyth County, Virginia,
made this fretless banjo.*

Fig. 193. Banjo, wood and hide head,
1st quarter 20th century
*This plainly made five-string banjo
is from Northeast Tennessee. The hide
is stretched over a wooden hoop.*

Fig. 194. Dulcimer, soft wood, 35 x 8 inches, 4th quarter 19th century
*This teardrop shaped dulcimer was made by Testerman, from Smyth
County, Virginia. It has scrolled F holes, no strum hollow, 4 strings
anchored with a metal tailpiece, wooden friction pegs, and a scrolled
reeded neck. It was a gift from the maker to regional historian,
Lewis Summers.*

Fig. 195. Dulcimer, walnut and cherry, 30½ inches, 1st quarter 20th century
Melton was the maker's name of note for this Lee County, Virginia, dulcimer. It is half-fretted, with factory pegs and numerous drilled sound holes.

Fig. 196. Dulcimer, poplar, cherry,
pine, and walnut, 41½ inches,
4th quarter 19th century
*The maker of this dulcimer, which was
found in Hawkins County, Tennessee, is
unknown. The tailpiece is made of sheet
metal, and the instrument is full fretted
and will accommodate six strings.*

Fig. 197. Dulcimer
*This unusual half-bout dulcimer,
carved from a single piece of wood,
is from Greene County, Tennessee.*

Bibliography

Beasley, Ellen. "Tennessee Cabinetmakers and Chairmakers through 1840." In *Antiques in Tennessee* (reprinted from *Antiques,* Aug., Sept., Oct., and Dec. 1971), n.p.

Brackman, Barbara. *Clues in the Calico: A Guide to Identifying and Dating Antique Quilts.* McLean, Va.: EPM Publications, Inc., 1989.

Comstock, H. E. *The Pottery of the Shenandoah Valley Region.* Winston Salem, N.C.: Museum of Early Southern Decorative Arts, 1994.

Comstock, Helen. *American Furniture: Seventeenth, Eighteenth, and Nineteenth Century Styles.* New York: Viking Press, 1962.

Crawford, Barbara, and Royster Lyle Jr. *Rockbridge County Artists and Artisans.* Charlottesville: University Press of Virginia, 1995.

Cultural Heritage Project Archive, William King Regional Arts Center, Abingdon, Va.

Dorman, John Frederick. *The Prestons of Smithfield and Greenfield in Virginia.* Louisville, Ky.: Filson Club, 1982.

Egloff, Keith, and Deborah Woodward. *First People: The Early Indians of Virginia.* Richmond, Va.: Virginia Department of Historic Resources, 1992.

Espenshade, Christopher T. *Potters on the Holston: Historic Pottery Production in Washington County, Virginia.* Morgantown, W.Va.: Skelly and Loy, Inc., 2002.

Historical Society of Washington County (Virginia). "King and Lynn Inventory, 1809." Publication ser. 2, no. 15, Aug. 1978.

———. "King and Lynn Inventory, Continued." Publication ser. 2, nos. 16 and 17, 1991.

McConnell, Catherine S. *Sänders Säga.* McClure Press, 1972.

Montgomery, Charles. *American Furniture, The Federal Period in the Henry Francis du Pont Winterthur Museum.* New York: Viking Press, 1966.

Moore, J. Roderick. "Earthenware Potters Along the Great Road in Virginia and Tennessee." *Antiques,* Sept. 1983, 528–37.

———. "Wythe County, Virginia, Punched Tin: Its Influence and Imitators." *Antiques,* Sept. 1984, 601–13.

———. *Great Road Style: Decorative Arts of Southwest Virginia, 1860–1940.* WKRAC exhibition guide, 1999.

Napps, Klell B. "Traditional Pottery in Washington County, Virginia and Sullivan County, Tennessee." Historical Society of Washington County (Virginia) Publication Series 11 (10), 1972, 3–16.

Nave, Robert T. *A History of the Iron Industry in Carter County to 1860.* Johnson City, Tenn.: Robert T. Nave, 1998.

Nutting, Wallace. *Furniture Treasury.* Vol. 3. New York: MacMillan, 1933.

Pain, Howard. *The Heritage of Country Furniture.* New York: Van Nostrand Reinhold Co., 1978.

Rouse, Parke, Jr. *The Great Wagon Road: From Philadelphia to the South.* Richmond, Va.: Dietz Press, 1995.

Smith, Samuel D., and Stephen T. Rogers. *A Survey of Historic Pottery Making in Tennessee.* Nashville, Tenn.: Division of Archaeology, Tennessee Department of Conservation, 1979.

Summers, Lewis Preston. *History of Southwest Virginia, 1746–1870, Washington County, 1777–1870.* Richmond, Va.: J. L. Hill Printing Company, 1903.

United States Agricultural Census, Southwest Virginia, 1850, 1870.

United States Manufacturer's Census, Southwest Virginia, 1870.

United States Population Census, 1850, 1860, 1870, for Buchanan, Dickenson, Lee, Russell, Scott, Smyth, Tazewell, Washington and Wise counties in Va., and for Carter, Hawkins, Johnson, Sullivan, Washington counties in Tenn.

Williams, Derita Coleman, and Nathan Harsh. *The Art and Mystery of Tennessee Furniture and Its Makers Through 1850.* Nashville, Tenn.: Tennessee Historical Society, Tennessee State Museum Foundation, 1988.

Young, Namuni Hale. *Art and Furniture of East Tennessee.* Knoxville, Tenn.: East Tennessee Historical Society, 1997.

William King Regional Arts Center Exhibitions Guides

12,000 Years Before the "White Man": An Exhibition of Indian and Settler Art and Artifacts From Southwest Virginia. 1996.

Great Road Style: Decorative Arts of Southwest Virginia, 1780–1860. 1998.

Great Road Style: Decorative Arts of Southwest Virginia, 1860–1940. 1999.

Great Road Style: Decorative Arts of Northeast Tennessee, 1780–1940. 2000.

Stories on Canvas: Portraiture from Southwest Virginia and Northeast Tennessee, 1780–1940. 2000.

Her Wooden Canvas: The Carvings of Mabel Barrow Kreger. 2002.

Virginia Clothed: Commerce and Fashion Along the Great Wagon Road, 1780–1900. 2002.

# Index

Italicized page numbers refer to illustrations